POWER

FOR THE

PEOPLE

POWER

FOR THE

PEOPLE

PROTECTING STATES' ENERGY POLICY
INTERESTS IN AN ERA OF DEREGULATION

MARY M. TIMNEY

M.E.Sharpe
Armonk, New York
London, England

Library of Congress Cataloging-in-Publication Data

Timney, Mary M.
    Power for the people : protecting states' energy policy interests in an era of deregula-
tion / by Mary M. Timney.
        p. cm.
    Includes bibliographical references and index.
    ISBN 0-7656-1148-1 (cloth : alk. paper)
    1. Energy policy—United States. 2. Energy policy—United States—States. 3. Electric
utilities—Government policy—United States. 4. Electric utilities—Government policy—
United States—States. 5. Electric utilities—Deregulation—United States. I. Title.
HD9502.U52 T56 2004
333.79′0973—dc22

                                                                                    2003023974

Printed in the United States of America

The paper used in this publication meets the minimum requirements of
American National Standard for Information Sciences
Permanence of Paper for Printed Library Materials,
ANSI Z 39.48-1984.

MV (c)   10   9   8   7   6   5   4   3   2   1

To our grandchildren,
who will inherit the consequences
of policies that we make today

Contents

List of Tables and Figures

Tables

Figures

Preface

I began this project in the summer of 2001 while I was living in Hayward, California. As the electricity deregulation crisis unfolded, it demonstrated that states have many policy interests that are related to energy policy. When one of them is turned over to the market, the state loses control over all the others, including the price of basic electricity service. State energy policies, since the mid-1970s, have been designed to make sure that there is enough energy for all users in the state and for economic development, delivered at a price that all users can pay, and generated in ways that do not harm the state's environment.

Nowhere are these values more important than in California, where the natural beauty of the state's environment is as important to economic development as is the availability of sufficient supplies of electricity at reasonable prices. Deregulation promised lower prices, but policymakers overlooked the hidden costs of a restructured market where profits are the only interest. Indeed, it is this profit imperative that led to the crisis in the winter of 2001, where energy providers took advantage of policy weaknesses to garner huge profits as high as 100 percent over the previous year.

When electricity prices spiraled out of control and led to the bankruptcy filing of the state's largest utility, the state stepped in to regain control over the complex of policy interests. Chief among these was reinstituting energy efficiency programs to encourage Californians to conserve electricity. They were so successful that electricity demand dropped by more than 10 percent. In our house, we turned off lights and remote controls. I worked on this manuscript by natural daylight as much as possible. We saved more than 15 percent of our electricity that summer and earned a rebate for our efforts. It was not difficult; in fact, we tried to live as the Europeans do where bright lighting is far from the norm.

In this book I have provided research on state energy policy over a thirty-year period that documents the values on which those policies are based. I began this project with a relatively open mind about deregulation and gathered considerable information about it in an attempt to understand the positive arguments for dismantling a regulatory structure that always seemed to work pretty well. I used the California experience as a case study of deregulation in general.

I have also attempted to put electricity deregulation in the broader contexts of regulatory deregulation and the privatization of government movement. In doing so, I demonstrate that the interests of the market and the state are based on different values and are in fundamental conflict. While the state values people and acts to moderate impacts on the least of them, the market values profits alone, regardless of impacts on some of the people or small business. I conclude, then, that states must recognize this conflict and structure deregulation policies so that they can balance the interests of both the people and the market. Without such a balance, the people will always lose.

Like all authors, I had the support of many people on this project. First, I thank my graduate students at California State University, Hayward, especially Rachel Levine, who did research for chapter 7 and wrote much of it; Jack Kenny, who developed a bibliography on California deregulation that was enormously helpful in getting me started; my regulatory policy class, who read the first draft of the manuscript; and all those students whose encouragement that year meant so much to me. I also thank Karena Garbesi for data and insights on electricity in California and Dick Ottinger, former U.S. Representative and "father" of the Public Utility Regulatory Policy Act, who shared his extensive e-mail energy file with me. Thanks also to Harry Briggs, my editor, who waited too patiently for the manuscript, and several friends who provided ongoing encouragement—especially Alan Knapp and Paul Fanning, Camilla Stivers, Ralph Hammel, Al Hyde, and Dale Krane. Above all I thank my husband, Mike Monfils, whose support for this project and my career have meant more than I can ever express.

POWER

FOR THE

PEOPLE

1

Introduction

Energy has become an important feature of national and state policymaking over the past thirty-plus years. From 1859, when the first oil well was drilled in Titusville, Pennsylvania, to the early 1970s, national energy policy focused on finding new supplies of oil anywhere in the world and enabling American companies to produce increasing amounts of energy to fuel the nation's economic growth. As domestic oil sources dwindled, American companies opened new fields in Venezuela and the Middle East. Imported oil was so cheap that policies had to be developed to protect American companies. Two major policies before 1973 were (1) the oil depletion allowance granted to oil producers that gave them tax breaks for pumping oil out of the ground and (2) minimum prices for oil sold in the United States set at a rate that made expensive domestic oil competitive with the cheaper oil coming from the Persian Gulf.[1] Energy policy amounted, then, to protecting the interests of the energy producers and ensuring a growing supply of low-priced energy.

The first comprehensive national energy policy was developed during the Ford administration in the mid-1970s, as the result of an energy "crisis" brought on by an embargo of oil exports imposed by the Organization of Petroleum Exporting Countries (OPEC), led by states in the Persian Gulf. The oil embargo awakened Americans to the fact of national dependence on foreign sources of energy and to the national security implications of this dependency. President Gerald Ford appointed Vice President Nelson Rockefeller to develop a plan for energy independence that would protect America's national security interests while assuring the availability of domestic sources of energy to keep the national economic engine running.

The notion of energy policy at the state level has a relatively brief history. Until the 1970s, states did not have a central focus on energy as a policy issue. States' energy interests were primarily concerned with public utility regulation, managing so-called natural monopolies of electricity and natural gas to prevent predatory pricing and ensure adequate supplies for residents and businesses. States that had energy producing industries were more likely to enact laws that protected those industries in the national economy. For the most part, however, states did not develop energy policy because there was no need for it. Energy was abundant and cheap in the United States. So long as the supply of all energy sources was equally available to all states the only real policy issue was how to set prices for regulated utilities that ensured them a reasonable profit while keeping prices down for consumers.

In the 1970s, when energy prices suddenly increased as the result of manipulation of oil prices on the world market, many U.S. states faced serious social and financial problems. In cold regions, low-income people were hit with both high heating costs and poorly maintained houses that leaked heat, which necessitated higher energy use. In hot regions, skyrocketing prices for electricity made air conditioning prohibitively expensive. The elderly poor were badly affected by both temperature extremes as they struggled to pay utility bills out of low fixed incomes.

Energy prices also affected businesses and governmental operations as the increasing costs had to be incorporated into their budgets. Energy-producing states, like Texas and Alaska, enjoyed huge budget surpluses because of royalties paid for in-state oil production. Energy-poor states, like Wisconsin and Minnesota, suffered shortages of oil and natural gas, which had a negative impact on their ability to retain and attract business in the state. It became clear across the country that all states needed comprehensive energy policies to find ways to protect the interests of all the people, reduce the costs of energy use as much as possible, and develop ways to protect against supply shortages.

States were encouraged and aided in these efforts throughout the 1970s by the Ford and Carter administrations. In 1975, the Federal Energy Administration, established by the Ford administration, began the process of developing a national energy policy. There were two foci at that time: (1) energy independence to protect the United States from price manipulation on the international market and (2) energy conservation on a massive scale. The mantra of the Ford Administration in those days was "A barrel of oil saved is cheaper than a new barrel."[2] It was widely recognized at that time, across all political ideologies, that the United States wasted large amounts of energy through inefficient industrial processes, poor building and residential construction, and, most emphatically, transportation. Automobiles in 1975 averaged fuel efficiencies far below 20 miles per gallon and public transportation was unavailable in many cities in the country.[3] U.S. policymakers looked seriously at energy conservation for the first time and also saw its considerable benefits for improving environmental protection, a major policy issue in the early 1970s.

The Energy Policy and Conservation Act of 1975 provided grants to states to establish their own energy offices to promote energy conservation through public information campaigns. States were required to develop plans to reduce their energy consumption by 5 percent below the expected level without conservation. Other federal programs gave grants to states to implement energy conservation in public buildings, low-income housing, schools, and hospitals. Gas and electric utilities, regulated by the states, were required to develop programs to encourage their customers to conserve. These "demand-side management" programs were hugely successful in California until 1996 when electricity deregulation was enacted.

States responded to these initiatives in different ways. Generally, those states that are net energy importers and more vulnerable to price shocks, such as Wisconsin and Minnesota, were more likely to develop policies that reduced energy demand. States with indigenous energy resources, like Texas and Alaska, or producers of surplus electricity that could be sold to the grid, such as Indiana and Ohio, were less likely to focus on conservation except to provide energy subsidies for low-income residents. Nonetheless, by 1980, there was a broad consensus across the country in support of energy conservation (Kash and Rycroft 1984). By the end of the 1970s, conservation had provided more new energy to the nation than any other source (Kash and Rycroft 1984: 238). In California, where energy demand was growing faster than supply, Pacific Gas and Electric Company became a national leader in conservation and demand-side management programs.

All states have an interest in ensuring that they will have access to stable supplies of energy at reasonable prices for all users. The states' three primary energy policy interests are the state economy, the ability of all residents to pay utility bills, and protection of the state's environment.[4] Utility costs are interwoven throughout the fabric of the state economy. High utility costs reduce a company's competitiveness by increasing operating costs. These impacts are most serious for small businesses whose profit margins are narrow. Higher costs also lead to higher prices for consumer goods and services, raising the cost of living in the state in relation to its neighbors. Thus, high utility costs can force a state into economic decline and make it a less desirable place in which to live.

The impact of high energy costs is felt most heavily by lower-income residents. In colder climates, inability to pay high heating bills has led to deaths, particularly among the poor elderly. Heat waves in the summer where air conditioning is prohibitively expensive can also increase the death rate among the poor and elderly on fixed incomes. In other cases, poor people must make difficult choices between spending money on electricity or heating fuel and other necessities. Beginning in the 1970s, many states developed programs to subsidize energy bills and to weatherize the homes of low-income citizens to reduce their energy usage and costs.

The cost of government operations also rises with higher utility bills. Government buildings, schools, hospitals, universities, and nonprofit institutions all operate on limited budgets. When funds must be diverted to energy costs, spending on other programs must be curtailed. States and cities do not have the ability to operate with a budget deficit and therefore must cut spending on other programs in order to pay higher electricity bills.

The interests of the states, then, are simple. They need a stable supply of energy—electricity, natural gas, and heating fuel—at a reasonable price so that businesses can operate efficiently and residents can afford to manage their households, and it should be produced in such a way that the state's environmental assets are least affected. Price spikes in energy costs, including transportation fuels, require a shift of resources from other spending and saving that could eventually lead to a downward spiral of the state's economy. In California, exorbitant market prices for electricity in the winter of 2001 resulted in a massive shift of state wealth to a handful of electricity traders and producers outside of the state. As a consequence, the state budget, which had been forecast to increase spending due to a projected multibillion-dollar surplus, had to be cut back. The surplus was used instead by the governor to purchase electricity on the open market in an effort to rescue financially strapped public utilities from economic collapse.

Deregulation and the Move to the Free Market

During the late 1970s, there was a movement in the country to abolish government regulation of industry. Economists called for deregulation to get government out of the business world and permit the free market to provide consumers with choices of products and services, at prices they were willing to pay. The focus of the deregulation movement was general across the economy. The first industries to be deregulated were transportation, telecommunications, and natural gas. By the early 1980s, the airline and trucking industries had been deregulated and AT&T had been broken up by court order. Natural gas was partially deregulated during the Carter administration and fully deregulated after Ronald Reagan took office in 1981.

The oil companies called for deregulation after the OPEC cartel raised international oil prices in the early 1970s. Oil prices in the United States had been regulated since the 1920s in order to protect domestic producers from cheaper imports. This provided a price floor below which oil prices could not fall. In 1973, when imported oil became more expensive, domestic price floors became caps. Oil resources in the United States were declining and oil left in the ground was too expensive to recover so long as the price caps remained in place. Because a major focus of energy policy in that decade was to free the United States from imported oil—energy independence—industry lobbyists pressed for deregulation of oil prices so that domestic prices for all oil would rise and domestic supplies would then be increased because of market demand. By the end of the decade, however, conservation and economic slowdown had so reduced demand for energy that oil prices on the market began to fall to pre-1973 levels.

Deregulation as a general policy gained more prominence toward the end of the decade. Economist Alfred Kahn, chairman of the Civil Aeronautic Board, pushed for deregulation of air transportation and trucking, including the dissolution of his own agency. Industries gathered political support against the new social regulations—environmental protection, consumer protections, occupational safety and health—that increased their costs of production while giving them no direct benefits. Conservative ideologues were also gaining political ground and deregulation was one of the planks in their platform.

When President Ronald Reagan took office in 1981, much of the energy policy infrastructure established during the Carter administration was dismantled. Oil and natural gas prices were deregulated, national energy policy was turned over to the free market, and the emphasis shifted from reducing demand to increasing supply. During his campaign, the president had pledged to eliminate the Department of Energy, which had been established only a few years earlier. He could not develop the political support in Congress to do so. Instead, the administration transformed the department's mission and its budget. The mission turned from demand-side management to allowing the market to determine supply. Conservation programs were slashed—from $1 billion annually to $10 million in 1983, a 90 percent cut (Davis 1983: 183). The department was refocused on aiding in the buildup of national defense and the portion of the budget devoted to nuclear weapons was increased. The focus of the Department of Energy was fundamentally changed through executive order, leaving it a shadow of its former self. Reagan, thus, accomplished his objective without congressional approval.

As energy policy shifted from demand to supply at the federal level, what then happened to the national consensus that Kash and Rycroft had documented? Did the states discontinue their programs and were their energy policy interests still met? For the most part, the answers to these questions are no and yes. States continued to fund their energy offices, initially using "oil overcharge" allotments, monies awarded to the states by court decisions after finding that the major oil companies had overcharged customers during the 1970s. Most states received several million dollars each year from 1986 to 1993. Many states used these funds to continue operating energy offices and to fund various energy management programs, including weatherization projects and low-income energy assistance grants. A study of seventeen Midwestern states in 1991 found that the general consensus of state interests was still very much in place (Bailey 1993). This study is described in chapter 3.

The Deregulation Juggernaut

As late as 1993, most states were still focused on protecting their primary energy policy interests: affordability, ample supply, and environmental protection. Then came deregulation. The National Energy Act of 1992 established the framework for the development of a national electricity market and created the possibility for consumer choice among electricity providers. Companies such as Enron Corporation and Reliant Corporation in Texas and Duke Energy Corporation in North Carolina became energy brokers that could facilitate the marketing of electricity throughout North America. The availability of consumer choice promised to lead to lower prices for electricity as consumers, in theory, would shop around to find the cheapest provider. States came under increasing pressure from industries and big energy users to deregulate electricity so that prices could fall.

In 1996, California became the first state in the country to deregulate electricity. Industry lobbyists convinced a conservative Republican governor and a Democrat majority legislature that the price of electricity in the state was artificially high because of inefficient regulation. If companies could not have a choice of providers, it was argued, they would move their operations to a neighboring state where prices were lower. To keep them in the state, electricity must be turned over to the free market so that large users could shop for the lowest prices. Deregulation was approved unanimously by both houses of the California legislature and then-Governor Pete Wilson signed the bill with great confidence that his own political fortunes as a potential presidential candidate would be improved as a result.

Customer electricity choice for residents and small businesses began in 1998. Small customers who did not choose an alternative supplier remained customers of the three independently owned utilities—Pacific Gas and Electric in the north, San Diego Gas and Electric and Southern California Edison in the south. Los Angeles, Sacramento, and a few other cities have municipal electricity generation and have lobbied to be excluded from the deregulation framework. Three years later, the state's deregulated electricity prices rose to previously unimagined highs and the utilities faced bankruptcy. The free-market dream of cheaper electricity had turned into a nightmare of outrageously high prices accompanied by rolling blackouts during the winter and spring of 2001. Alternative electricity providers abandoned consumers as the major utilities in the state grew unable to pay their market prices. Ultimately the state stepped in, became the primary electricity buyer for the utilities, and entered into negotiations with the utilities to buy their transmission lines. Calls for re-regulation were heard from every corner of the state, and included some of the strongest voices who had advocated deregulation. Other states watched the debacle with a mix of smugness and trepidation. Californians were portrayed as energy wastrels, wallowing in their hot tubs while their computers ran 24/7. The crisis was blamed on flaws in the legislation that established price "caps" and forbade the utilities to enter into long-term contracts. There was growing fear that it could happen elsewhere.

The march to deregulation stopped. States that had been moving toward it pulled back, others delayed implementation. As of February 2003, fewer than half of the states (twenty-four) had enacted restructuring legislation. Of these, however, seven had delayed implementing retail access and one, California, had suspended restructuring completely (Energy Information Administration, January 2002). By June 2003, no new state had begun deregulating electricity.

Absent from the analyses of this failure was any discussion of flaws in the concept of deregulation itself as a public policy. In California, policymakers focused primarily on the excesses of the market and alleged price gouging by the electricity brokers. Protectors of deregulation, on the other hand, scorned state lawmakers for developing a "flawed" deregulation policy that prohibited the utilities from entering into long-term contracts to purchase electricity, leaving them captives of the spot market. Had the utilities had access to long-term contracts, it was argued, they would not have been caught in the dynamics of a normal and volatile free-market system. A true free market in electricity would, in the long run, produce supplies at a price consumers would be willing to pay, they said. Thus, one might conclude that the crisis was the result of either a legislative failure or a market failure or both.

Another conclusion, however, just as plausible, is that it was a huge market success. The market acted just the way free markets are supposed to, pricing scarce commodities higher as demand increases and the purchaser's ability to pay becomes more uncertain. At one point during the height of the crisis, when the state took over purchasing electricity for the utilities, energy providers charged $3,880 for a megawatt-hour of electricity that normally sold for about $300. A surcharge of $3,104 was built into the price as a credit penalty because of fears that the utilities would renege on payments (Geissinger 2001). The companies, and eventually the state, had no choice but to agree to pay. Electricity is not an optional commodity in American life, and we will generally pay whatever it takes to keep the lights on.

This is the central fault in deregulation and other mechanisms for privatizing government services. As long as utilities were regulated as natural monopolies, the states were able to protect their primary energy policy interests—affordability and adequate supply. Those interests are of little concern to the market, however, which has only one interest:

making the largest profit possible as quickly as possible. It is this fundamental difference in focus that makes the market a questionable mechanism for providing universal public services and serving the public interest. Wholesale devolution of the state's policy interests to the market, as is done with deregulation, results in loss of political control over essential public policies at the expense of the state's economy and quality of life.

Purpose of the Book

This book examines state energy policy as it has developed since 1973 and documents the primary interests that the states have held for their own energy policies. It builds on a study of the early 1990s that examined developments in state energy policy during the 1980s in the absence of national energy policy direction (Bailey 1993). That study documented the states' priorities in energy policy at the time. During the summer of 2001, a comprehensive study of state Web sites was conducted to update this information, and it determined that state energy policy priorities had not shifted despite the emphasis on deregulation during the 1990s. California, when faced with extreme market prices, acted to protect its primary energy policy interests.

The main thrust of my analysis is on deregulation as a mechanism for achieving state energy policy goals and the question of whether the market can truly meet the complex policy interests of the state. The California case raises the following questions, among others: Is the California experience an aberration or just business as usual for the market? Can any market be truly free when there are only a few providers? Is electricity a natural monopoly after all? Was this a political failure or a market failure? Are market interests and state interests in fundamental conflict? Did the market actually work too well in California?

There are no simple answers to these questions. They are, however, important issues for public policy, in general. The pressure to get government off the backs of business and to privatize public interests continues across all sectors. Electricity is used here as a powerful example of the flaws of free-market ideology for achieving public-policy objectives. My central argument is that the assumptions on which deregulation policy was made do not serve the complex interests of the people, nor can they. The market cannot meet the needs of all the people—only the largest and most demanding consumers really get a choice—and the related policy interests of the state fall far behind the interests of the market. The book, then, is also an examination of free-market ideology as the basis for public policy. My aim is to demonstrate that there is a role for government that is superior to the market in the provision of services to all the people, not just the biggest, richest, and smartest.

Chapter 2 provides an overview of energy policy history in the United States from roughly World War I to 2001 and of the energy policy proposed by the George W. Bush administration. This history reveals that government policy has long protected the interests of the energy producers for four of the five primary energy sources—oil, natural gas, nuclear, and electricity. Only coal has never been subsidized, and, in fact, over the past fifty years, policies have been developed to limit its use because of its negative health and environmental effects. Comprehensive energy policy in the United States was not developed until the last three decades of the twentieth century. During this period, energy policy moved from the national to the state levels and from tax subsidies to increase energy production prior to the 1970s, to tax credits to increase supply through efficiency and demand management in the Carter administration, to deregulation of energy resources to increase supply in the Reagan administration. The cycle was completed with the Bush II administration's deemphasis on conservation and demand-side management and renewed emphasis on: (1) expanding the supply of fossil fuel-based energy resources in the twenty-first century; (2) relaxing environmental protection laws so that more coal generators could be built quickly; and (3) restoring nuclear power as a desirable source of electricity.

Chapter 3 provides an overview of state energy policies from 1975 to 1995, the year that California enacted electricity restructuring policy. It describes the states' problems in the 1970s as they tried to adjust to rapidly rising energy prices and cushion their citizens and businesses from the impacts of these costs. The results of a study of seventeen Midwestern states at the beginning of the 1990s documents those states' activities in energy policy development during the 1980s when the national energy policy developed during the Ford and Carter administrations had been dismantled. The message coming out of Washington in the 1980s was that there was no need for a national energy policy. Natural gas had been deregulated and the OPEC cartel had collapsed as oil prices fell, in large measure as the result of widespread energy

conservation by Americans during the 1970s. The Reagan administration's policy at the time was to let the market develop energy policy
so that the dynamic of supply and demand would dictate the need for
new energy sources and technology as prices rose.

The study found that the states in this sample did not adopt this philosophy but continued to develop their own energy policies based on the
individual needs of their residents and businesses. States had experienced many negative impacts of market fluctuations during the 1970s.
The poor and elderly suffered disproportionately from sharp increases
in heating and cooling costs. Small businesses, nonprofits, and governments themselves were forced to devote greater budgetary resources to
utility costs. Uncertain energy supplies, in general, had a negative impact on state economies resulting in migration of businesses to energy-
rich states. States worked toward developing policies that would ensure
a dependable supply of energy at affordable prices for all users, delivered in ways that protected the state's environmental quality. Documen-
tation of these states' complex policy interests provides a base for
analyzing the current interests outlined in state energy policies.

Chapter 4 describes the push for restructuring the electricity industry and deregulation of electricity pricing in the 1990s. An examination of the history of electricity regulation provides a look at the
development of regulatory roles of both the states and the federal government. The chapter also provides an overview of major federal legislation that eventually led the states to implement electricity
restructuring and deregulation policy. The political issues involved in
restructuring independently owned public utilities are discussed, including such issues as amortization of the costs of stranded assets,
retail wheeling, and consumer protection. The social and environmental costs of restructuring are also considered.

The California experience in the winter of 2000–2001 is used as a
case study of electricity deregulation in chapter 5. The case documents
the development of electricity deregulation policy in California, the main
features of the legislation, and the political dynamics of the passage of
the legislation. A detailed description of the electricity crisis in California from summer 2000 to summer 2001 is followed by an analysis of the
factors associated with this policy failure.

Chapter 6 examines the deregulation experiences of other states. The
policies in several states, particularly Pennsylvania, New York, and Ohio,
are compared to California's. Strengths and weaknesses of state policies

and their experiences with deregulation are examined along with evidence of the lessons other states learned from the California experience.

Chapter 7 looks at whether state energy policy interests changed with deregulation and how the states themselves see their role in setting policy for energy supply and prices today. A study of the Web sites of all fifty states was conducted and a content analysis was used to identify the primary interests that are articulated in describing energy policy at the state level. The findings are compared to the findings from the 1990 study and analyzed to determine whether there are significant differences between the interests of regulated and deregulated states.

Chapter 8 provides a general discussion of state interests versus market interests. It establishes a framework for examining whether the market can meet the complex policy interests of the state or if, instead, the market actually overwhelms state policy interests through distorting incentives and encouraging overconsumption. The inability of the market to reduce demand—a dominant state energy policy interest—except through predatory pricing is discussed along with the policy issue of growth in supply versus reduction in demand through conservation and efficiency. It looks at the American lifestyle and distorted incentives to consume more energy that come from the market. A fundamental focus of this chapter is on the question of whether the market really worked in electricity deregulation in the way that free market theory claims. What are the limits of the free market in meeting policy interests or providing public goods?

Accepting that the deregulation genie cannot be put back into its bottle at this point, Chapter 9 examines the possibility of balancing state energy policy interests and market interests by designing policies that use the best part of market mechanisms while protecting the interests of the state. What was good about regulation? What is good about deregulation? Can two failures—policy and market—make a success? Is it possible to blend or balance public and private interests? New roles for federal and state regulators are defined by deregulation. The failure of the Federal Energy Regulatory Commission (FERC) to protect California's energy policy interests is examined.

Chapter 10 considers the aftermath of the California crisis and the future of electricity deregulation policy itself. The collapse of the Enron Corporation, the decline of other energy producers, and the evidence of market manipulation in California must lead to a reconsideration of electricity restructuring as public policy. Yet the electricity industry has been transformed despite the reality that over one-half of the states have not deregulated. As the FERC attempts to make restructuring a national mandate, states are moving to protect their policy interests and even to re-regulate. I argue that the FERC must assume a new role post-deregulation to restore the federal-state partnership and work to protect the interests of the states in the deregulated market.

The chapter includes a philosophical discussion of whether, in fact, the market really works for all the people and the role of the state in ensuring that it does. I argue that the states can take from the California case important lessons about the necessity to develop state energy policies that protect citizens from the vagaries of a wildcat energy market.

The conclusion in Chapter 11 considers the proper role of government and the proper role of the market in providing public policy in a democratic polity where citizens are more than just consumers. It briefly considers the purpose of economics and questions whether Adam Smith himself would approve of the way that the free market operates in the United States today. Would he have seen the differences between producing and selling widgets and the provision of a necessity of modern life through the market? Finally, the question of who serves the people is posed. The answer, of course, depends on one's own belief in the value of democratic governance and one's skepticism of the ability of the free market to produce a society that is fair and just and inclusive of all the people, not just the richest, cleverest and most well born.

Chapter 12 is an epilogue that briefly considers the role of deregulation in the electricity blackout of August 2003.

2

A Brief History
of U.S. Energy Policy

Before 1970, U.S. energy policy was effectively oil and gas policy. The United States did not have a comprehensive energy policy. Until the "energy crisis" in 1973, precipitated by the Organization of Petroleum Exporting Countries (OPEC) oil embargo that drove up prices on the world market, energy policy was largely a function of federal government policy in relation to five energy sources: oil, natural gas, electricity, coal, and nuclear power. Most policy was designed primarily to support the health and wealth of the energy producers—specifically oil, natural gas, and nuclear power—in the name of the greater public interest, especially national defense and economic development. Coal is the only fuel that has not enjoyed government protection and support, although there have been three different government-sponsored efforts to develop synthetic oil and gas (synfuels) from coal (see Vietor 1984).

The goal of pre-1973 national energy policy was a commitment to ever-larger quantities of energy at ever-lower prices. Policies focused on energy fuel production to ensure abundant, stable, low-cost energy supplies. "Cheap, abundant energy was the basis of social and political stability. It provided the foundation for economic growth and for the acceptance of common societal rules" (Kash and Rycroft 1984: 47).

Energy in all its forms was cheap in the United States. Indigenous supplies of fossil fuels allowed the nation's economy to grow robustly. When domestic supplies of oil began to decline after World War I, imports from the Middle East became available. In 1933, the Standard Oil Company of California (Socal) negotiated a 60-year agreement with the Saudi Arabian government for exclusive rights to the country's eastern oil region. Socal established the Californian Arabian Standard Oil Company which was renamed the Arabian American Oil Company, Aramco, in 1944. By 1948, Socal had sold interests in the venture to Standard Oil of New Jersey (later Exxon) and Socony Vacuum (later Mobil) (Saudia Arabian Information Resource, November 9, 2002). In an extraordinary deal in the early 1950s, the State Department and the Treasury Department agreed to credit taxes that U.S. companies earned pumping oil in Saudi Arabia, in order to bolster the Saudi economy and establish an important ally in the region. This agreement was known as "The Golden Gimmick" (Davis 1978: 75). Because Middle Eastern oil at the time was also very cheap, domestic U.S. oil producers successfully lobbied for the establishment of price caps that set a higher price for imported oil so that domestic oil could be competitive. Oil producers also received favorable tax consideration through the oil depletion allowance. This vehicle was in essence a subsidy of domestic oil companies by the U.S. government.

Energy use grew in concert with the post–World War II U.S. economy. By the early 1970s, Americans were accustomed to paying much lower prices for energy than were consumers in other developed countries. A gallon of gasoline in the United States, pumped by an attendant who also checked the oil and washed the windows, sold for about 25 cents in 1972 and gas stations gave away premiums such as glassware to attract customers. Europeans and Japanese at the time paid the equivalent of $2–3 per gallon.

Because of the low prices, Americans were also accustomed to wasting considerable amounts of energy. Automobiles of the 1970s averaged fuel consumption of 10–12 miles per gallon or less. Cars of that era were large, roomy, and heavy. After World War II, public transportation systems across the country were dismantled or pared down. New suburban neighborhoods, built beyond the range of public transportation, spurred the increase in the use of personal automobiles to get to work, shops, and recreation destinations.

Buildings constructed from the 1950s to early 1970s were the least energy efficient since cave dwellings. High-rise office buildings had fixed single-pane windows and heating, ventilation, and cooling (HVAC) systems that were designed to be inefficient.[1] Tract housing was built with ill-fitting windows and doors and with no insulation, necessitating higher thermostat settings for heating and lower ones for cooling. Because electricity and natural gas bills were relatively low, most Americans gave little thought to the efficiency of the systems or the quality of housing construction. They simply raised the thermostat setting to compensate for drafts coming through the walls and windows. Indeed, builders of housing and office buildings depended on cheap energy to keep their construction costs affordable.

All of this changed in the 1970s when the OPEC cartel raised oil prices on the world market and the Iranian government placed an embargo on exports to the United States. By 1974, the Saudi Arabian government had taken back 60 percent of its oil fields.[2] Overnight the price of gasoline in the United States doubled and all other energy prices that were dependent on oil also increased dramatically. Known natural gas reserves in the United States were dwindling. Electricity power plants fueled by natural gas were shut down and oil-powered generators became increasingly expensive to operate. Electricity generated from coal was under pressure at the time because of new environmental protection laws governing air and water quality. The Clean Air Act Amendments of 1970 and the Water Pollution Control Act of 1972 imposed stringent controls on coal-burning power plants to reduce air pollutants— primarily sulfur dioxide and particulate matter or fly ash. Water contaminated with these pollutants and other by-products of burning coal was also strictly regulated. Midwestern companies, notably American Electric Power of Ohio and Indiana, developed tall stack technology that pushed pollution higher into the atmosphere to reduce the ambient pollution near the plants. Ten years later this upper-atmosphere pollution was identified as the major source of acid rain in New York and New England.

By 1975, however, coal had become the dominant choice for U.S. policymakers seeking to develop energy independence from foreign oil producers because of its abundant supply in the United States. As the Ford administration struggled to develop energy independence, domestic coal reserves became a central element in the emerging policy. Known U.S. coal reserves were as substantial at the time as oil reserves in Saudi Arabia. Interest in expanding coal production by as much as 300 percent led to the Carter administration's funding of research and development of synthetic oil and natural gas.

The focus of national energy policy had also changed dramatically. It was no longer possible to maintain price stability and continually increasing energy supplies given global energy market realities. The OPEC embargo focused the attention of policymakers on the relationship of energy supply to economic growth and on the national security implications of dependence on foreign sources of oil. Given that U.S.-controlled sources of oil were diminishing and known domestic deposits of natural gas were limited, the nation was forced to examine energy policy more broadly.

There was great uncertainty in the country about the future of domestic energy supplies and their availability to continue to fuel the economic growth engine. Recognition dawned throughout the country that energy is a precious resource that should not be wasted. The Nixon and Ford administrations began to develop a national energy policy for efficiency and conservation, based on the realization that saved energy is far cheaper than new energy development and it has a positive effect on the environment.[3] Gerald Ford's vice president, Nelson Rockefeller, headed a task force that developed a plan for energy independence that was heavily skewed toward increasing the production of coal. The Alaskan oil pipeline was also a significant factor in this discussion. Although some environmentalists opposed construction of the pipeline at all, the primary disagreement in the policy debate at that time was over the direction of the pipeline from Prudhoe Bay and whether it would cross Canada to terminate in the upper Midwestern states or cross Alaska to Prince William Sound where the oil would be loaded into tankers destined for refineries in California.

Nuclear power was seen as an important factor in national energy policy at that time. Atomic energy development is regulated by the federal government and originated as part of the Eisenhower administration's Atoms for Peace program. In the 1960s nuclear power had been championed as the cheapest way to generate electricity—so cheap that meters would be unnecessary. But in the 1970s, the costs to construct and operate nuclear power plants began to escalate. Protests against nuclear power plants by environmental and consumer activists made siting new plants increasingly difficult. In 1979, the nuclear power plant at Three Mile Island near Harrisburg, Pennsylvania, suffered a serious accident that led to a near meltdown of the reactor core. Further development of nuclear power ground to a halt throughout the country.

The goals of energy policy changed in the 1970s and so did the participants in the policy process. Prior to 1973, energy politics were dominated by the producers of fuels—oil, gas, and coal. Their goal was to develop policy that enabled them to produce as much as possible and expand their markets. Policies were designed to keep the producers satisfied for both economic growth and national security.

Where previous policy focused on abundance and cheapness, two

Table 2.1

New Participants in Energy Policy, Post-1973

Performance-motivated participants	Advocates of alternative technologies
	Energy system modelers
Impact-motivated participants	Short-term economic advocates
	Environmental and second-order impact activists (health, consumer)
Power-motivated participants	Domestic-policy actors (federal agencies, congressional committees, states)
	Foreign-policy actors Advocates for sociopolitical change

Source: Kash and Rycroft 1984: 89–106.

added goals shaped the development of new policy: cleanness and security (Kash and Rycroft 1984: 14–15). Cheapness became important because of huge price shocks in 1973 and 1978 that threatened the economy in nonproducing states and caused hardship for the poor and elderly. The environmental movement emphasized the polluting aspects of energy use based on fossil fuels.

Where policy had been designed by producers and Congress, the policy arena now included seven new participants who were not attached to any particular fuel (see Table 2.1). Energy policy became a contentious policy area for a variety of interests and no longer the sole province of fuel industry executives and their representatives in Congress. Performance-motivated participants included advocates of alternative energy technologies and energy system modelers who focused on resource limits and the need for technologies based on renewable resources. Impact-motivated participants included environmentalists, health professionals, and consumer advocates who were concerned about the impacts of energy development on the environment and human health as well as the consumer pocketbook. Power-motivated participants encompassed domestic-policy actors (federal agencies, congressional committees, the states) and foreign-policy actors as well as advocates for sociopolitical change (see Kash and Rycroft 1984: 89–106).

Energy production was increasingly seen as linked to foreign policy and U.S. dependence on foreign producers in the politically volatile

Middle East. For the first time, attempts were made to document all known reserves of energy sources in the United States and analysts developed models to estimate the lifetime of these supplies if user habits remain unchanged. Studies such as the Club of Rome's *The Limits to Growth* (Meadows et al. 1972) spurred the development of alternative energy sources. More importantly, this study began a serious discussion of the viability of the American dream and continual economic growth.

Conservation was the centerpiece of the emergent federal energy policy. For the first time, states, with the help of Washington, were required to develop their own energy policies focused on implementing plans to reduce energy use (see chapter 3). In addition, gas and electric utilities were required to develop programs to encourage their customers to conserve.

President Gerald Ford established two new energy agencies: the Federal Energy Administration and the Energy Research and Development Administration (ERDA). These agencies took some of the energy functions that had been housed in the Department of Interior and attempted to bring energy-related activities together with a focus on research and development of new energy resources. The ERDA was charged with promoting research on technology to synthesize oil and gas from coal and oil shale deposits. Ford also appointed Vice President Nelson Rockefeller to head an energy independence task force. The charge was to develop a plan to expand domestic energy production and reduce the nation's dependence on imported oil, particularly from the Middle East. The administration began to discuss the possibility of tripling the production of U.S. coal, the most abundant energy resource in the nation.

The 1976 election brought a stronger emphasis on energy efficiency. National energy policy was the major policy initiative in the early years of President Jimmy Carter's administration. Carter was a nuclear engineer who had gained a good reputation in the environmental community when governor of Georgia. He appointed several well-known environmental and consumer activists to high-level positions in his government. Shortly after his inauguration Carter appointed energy administrator James Schlesinger, who spearheaded the development of proposals for a comprehensive energy policy and a new cabinet Department of Energy (DOE). In a nationwide television address, Carter described the energy proposal as "the moral equivalent of war" (Davis 1978: 8). The new DOE was to develop (1) energy efficiency standards for automobiles and appliances; (2) building construction codes; (3) standards for thermostat settings in office buildings; and (4) tax incentives for energy conservation and solar energy purchases by homeowners and small businesses. The Synthetic Fuels Corporation was established to develop oil and natural gas production from coal and oil shale. The corporation set daily production goals of 500,000 barrels of oil-equivalent by 1987 and 2 million barrels of oil-equivalent by 1992 (Kash and Rycroft 1984: 274). The corporation was dismantled by the Reagan administration in the belief that the market would develop new fuels as the need developed.

Americans responded positively to these initiatives. Demand for small, fuel-efficient cars grew, particularly after a second OPEC-led price shock doubled gasoline prices again in 1978. The market for solar-energy products, efficient appliances, and insulation expanded. Construction standards for office buildings and housing reduced operating costs at the same time that they improved the quality of construction. By the early 1980s, growth in demand for electricity had declined significantly from the previous rate at which demand doubled about every ten years. Gasoline consumption in the United States dropped so much that the OPEC cartel collapsed and gasoline prices fell to pre-1978 levels in 1982. Thus, the evidence shows that there was widespread political support for energy policies that emphasized conservation and efficiency, across both major political parties, throughout the 1970s.

Policy development never occurs in a vacuum, however, and other initiatives often intersect with a given issue. In the late 1970s, the factor that began to influence energy policy most significantly was the movement toward deregulation. Oil and gas production were heavily regulated and that regulation was increasingly seen as a barrier to increasing supplies of affordable energy. Natural gas regulation set price caps on gas that was delivered to interstate markets while intrastate gas prices were not capped. Companies in Texas and Oklahoma sold their product in their own states and withheld gas from interstate markets, creating a shortage. The Carter Administration supported deregulation of natural gas via the Natural Gas Policy Act (NGPA) of 1978. The emphasis of this law was to allow prices of natural gas to rise gradually until 1985 through market mechanisms that accounted for the cost of exploration and the limited supply. At the time, known reserves of natural gas in the United States were dwindling and deeper wells had to be drilled at greater cost than the regulated prices allowed. The NGPA provided partial deregulation through a complex system of pricing "old" and "new" gas.

By 1980, however, the market had responded so effectively that the gas shortage disappeared (Kash and Rycroft: 210).

Electricity regulation had a different effect on pricing. Utility companies, regulated by the states, were generally allowed to request rate hikes that covered their costs of production plus a profit, the "cost plus" method. Many companies invested in expensive nuclear power plants with the blessings of the regulators. Because they could recover their costs no matter what fuel they used with existing technologies, utilities had little incentive to invest in the development of new technologies to generate electricity from nonfossil fuel sources, particularly renewable resources. In addition, because of the necessity to recoup their investments, most utilities were resistant to promoting energy conservation that would reduce their profits as well. It was difficult for companies that had traditionally increased profits by selling more to instead ask their customers to use less of their product. The major exception to this rule was the Pacific Gas and Electric Company (PG&E) in northern California, the nation's largest private utility in 1978. Faced with projections of continuing growth in demand and escalating construction costs, PG&E adopted "a far-reaching program of subsidies and incentives for conservation, cogeneration, and renewable energy" (Lee 1983: 190).

The National Energy Acts of 1978 forced utilities to get involved with renewables and conservation. First, the Public Utility Regulatory Policies Act (PURPA) required utilities to connect qualifying facilities (QFs) to their transmission grids and to purchase their power. Qualifying facilities are cogenerators and small power producers that produce electricity using renewable energy sources. The price was to be set at the cost savings to utilities for not having to build new capacity to generate the same amount of electricity (Brennan et al. 1996: 29). This section of the PURPA was designed to force the utilities to take renewable resource power generation seriously. Because it opened the grid for use by nonutility generators, however, it ultimately became the vehicle for electricity deregulation.

Second, the National Energy Conservation Act required utilities to establish a Residential Conservation Service that would provide information to consumers on ways to improve their energy efficiency, identification of conservation contractors, and financing assistance (Lee 1983: 186). The Energy Tax Act provided a 10 percent tax credit to generators using biomass, geothermal, wind, and solar energy; and, finally, the Power Plant and Industrial Fuel Use Act forbade the use of oil and natural gas in new power plants (Brennan et al. 1996: 30). Individual homeowners were also given tax incentives to encourage investment in both conservation projects, such as window replacement and caulking, and solar energy products.

The Federal Power Commission, which regulated wholesale natural gas and electricity prices, became the Federal Energy Regulatory Commission (FERC) in 1977. The FERCs charge was to manage wholesale energy markets, to ensure that utilities did open their transmission grids to QFs, and to protect consumers by ensuring that wholesale prices would be just and reasonable. When Ronald Reagan took office, he appointed Republicans to the majority of seats on the FERC and deregulation of natural gas was accelerated. The commission also revised regulations on transmission pipelines requiring them to accept gas from any source. This made the pipelines common carriers. (Davis 2001: 5)

The Carter conservation programs were phased out or eliminated in the Reagan administration, principally through the budget process rather than direct legislation. Tax incentives for conservation and solar energy tax credits were eliminated. The Synfuels Corporation was dismantled and research on alternative fuels was discontinued. Energy conservation programs in the DOE were phased out. The DOE's budget was directed toward nuclear weapons development as part of the administration's major defense buildup.

The administration embraced deregulation as a guiding principle wholeheartedly. The free-market philosophy of Milton Friedman and other neoconservative economists guided the administration's approach to public policy. In this atmosphere, energy was seen solely as a market. There was no reason for government to have a role in developing new energy technologies, it was argued. The competitive forces of American ingenuity coupled with the principle of supply and demand would stimulate the market to provide energy supplies at the appropriate time and at the appropriate price. In this conception, there was no longer any need for government-mandated conservation programs because the market would bring prices into an equilibrium that would send the proper signals to consumers as supplies rose and fell. If prices spiked because of shortages, then consumers would cut back—conserve—which would free up supply and bring prices back down.

In a demonstration of classic economic principles, the world market price of oil dropped sharply in the early 1980s because of oversupply. A number of factors led to the decline—conservation by American consumers, the U.S. recession, and the collapse of the OPEC cartel that had limited production during the 1970s. The price of gasoline in the United States fell below a dollar per gallon by 1983. Keeping gasoline prices down became an important element in national consumer policy and by 1993 the price of a gallon of gas was still lower than in 1982, despite several tax hikes in the interim.[4]

Prices for other energy sources—electricity and heating fuels—stabilized throughout the decade. Large new deposits of natural gas improved the supply picture for this fuel, easing concerns about availability of heating fuels and reducing upward pricing pressures. Electricity prices also stabilized in most places because of slower demand growth, the result of conservation, new building codes, and improved building materials and technology. Electricity rate hikes in many places were linked primarily to environmental requirements or earlier nuclear power construction decisions that had proved costly. By the early 1990s, energy prices when adjusted for inflation were generally lower than at the end of the 1970s. The amount of oil imported from abroad, however, increased during the 1980s (Davis 2001: 3).

Public and government interest in conservation also declined when the pressure of high prices disappeared. Large cars came back into fashion, thermostats were set higher in the winter and lower in the summer, natural gas grills and outdoor lighting returned to suburban neighborhoods, and new commercial and residential buildings were designed with grand open spaces and lots of glass. A general impression developed across the country that energy problems were over. This was shaken only slightly by the gasoline lines that sprang up at the beginning of the Persian Gulf War in 1989. Yet, because of improved building materials and construction methods, higher average performance of automobiles, and improved appliance efficiency, energy consumption did not increase proportionately.

During the 1980s, two major environmental problems related to energy production and use became prominent—acid deposition or rain and global warming, both of which are linked to fossil-fuel combustion. Several studies traced acid deposition in the United States and Canada to coal-burning power plants in Midwestern United States. The discovery of a hole in the ozone layer over the South Pole led to international policy efforts to halt the production of chlorofluorocarbons. There was a growing concern in the scientific community that fossil-fuel use was leading to climate change because of a buildup of carbon dioxide in the atmosphere. Extreme hot weather in the summer of 1988 led some reputable scientists to conclude that global warming had begun.

Despite the growing concern among the scientific community, environmental legislation was stalled during the Reagan administration because of the president's antipathy toward environmental protection. Democrats in Congress generally withheld any environmental legislation, including reauthorization of the Clean Air Act, for fear of a presidential veto that they did not have the votes to override. Bowing to pressure from the electric power industry, Reagan called for more study of both acid rain/deposition and global warming, despite the existence of several studies by reputable scientists that had already documented the probable causes. There was effectively no federal legislative activity in energy or environmental policy for the eight years of the Reagan administration.

During his campaign in 1988, George H.W. Bush pledged to become the "environmental president." Several new pieces of legislation were passed during his term of office. The Clean Air Act was finally amended in 1990, several years beyond the statutory requirement. The amendments required electricity generators to take significant measures to reduce acid emissions from power plants, including the installation of expensive technology to reduce pollution from high-sulfur coal use, the primary fuel of the midwestern power generators. For the first time, the act established market mechanisms to allow power companies to trade emissions on the market in order to reduce pollution in the most efficient and least costly way. It also encouraged the use of ethanol fuels in automobiles. A new law, the Intermodal Surface Transportation Efficiency Act of 1991, mandated that states improve transportation planning to reduce automobile emissions and included the threat of loss of highway funds if they failed to consider mass transportation.

One of the most influential pieces of legislation of this era, the National Energy Policy Act of 1992, focused on the efficient production and consumption of energy in the United States, restoring the federal-state consensus of the 1970s. While it was not a comprehensive energy policy as Carter's was, it sowed the seeds for the development of electricity restructuring and deregulation. Among the requirements of the act were the following:

1. States must incorporate energy-efficiency standards into commercial building codes and consider upgrading energy-efficiency codes for residential buildings.

2. The DOE must establish a voluntary home-energy rating system for comparing energy use in residential buildings.
3. Electric utilities must develop plans to promote energy efficiency using three approaches: (a) integrated resource planning, that would examine all possible energy fuel resources within their states, including solar, hydro, wind, geothermal, biomass, and so forth; (b) investments in demand-side management projects that were as profitable as investments in additional electricity generation; and (c) utility rate structures that were designed to encourage investments for efficiency in the generation, transmission, and distribution of electricity.

The act also (a) authorized cost-sharing grants to industry associations to support programs that improve energy efficiency in industry and (b) provided support for programs to improve efficiency ratings and standards. Federal agencies were required by 2000 to install all energy and water conservation measures in their buildings that had a payback period of less than ten years. Clearly, this law emphasized conservation and efficiency as national policy, a return to the consensus of the late 1970s.

Buried in the legislation, however, was the mechanism to free electricity from the confines of regulation. Title VII of the act reformed the Public Utility Holding Company Act (PUHCA) and established a class of exempt wholesale generators (EWGs) that could generate and sell electric power at wholesale without being subject to the regulatory restrictions mandated under PUHCA. The principal proponent of this concept was a good friend of President Bush—Kenneth Lay, CEO of the Enron Corporation of Houston, Texas. The Federal Energy Regulatory Commission was designated as the coordinator for EWGs, to assist them in gaining access to utility transmission lines in the same way that it did for QFs after 1978. The FERC was also granted the power to determine reasonable prices for transmission services (Kreith and Burmeister 1993: 356). Title VII is the mechanism that eventually made state deregulation of electricity possible although it is not evident from the record that this was the original intent of the legislation.

The 1992 National Energy Act also provided funding for state energy offices to pursue efficiency and conservation programs. By 2001, every state in the nation had a central energy office that was partially funded by the DOE. The act made a nod toward global climate change by requiring the DOE to conduct feasibility studies on the economic, energy, and environmental implications of stabilizing or reducing greenhouse gas emissions. Any future national energy strategies, moreover, were required to include a least-cost energy plan prepared by DOE to address economic, energy, social, and environmental costs and benefits.

The act was based on the Bush administration's National Energy Strategy, released in February 1991. The secretary of energy at the time, Admiral James D. Watkins, characterized it as "a strategy that, for the first time in our nation's history, lays a comprehensive foundation for a cleaner, more efficient and more secure energy future . . . a balanced approach to attaining that energy future through shared responsibility" (Kreith and Burmeister 1993: 8). This strategy included a proposal to open 600,000 hectares in the Arctic National Wildlife Refuge for oil and gas exploration and drilling. The proposal was met with intense opposition from environmentalists and Congress and was dropped from the final bill. It did not surface on the political agenda again until 2001, when George W. Bush took office.

The 1992 National Energy Act was framed around efficiency, conservation, and renewable energy sources with a clear understanding of the impacts of energy production on both air quality and global warming. President G.H.W. Bush, although avowing conservative Republican principles and free-market ideology, nonetheless supported a balanced approach to national energy policy that acknowledged the complex of policy issues intertwined with energy policy. His approach evoked traditional Republican ideals of conservation stemming from Teddy Roosevelt and Gifford Pinchot. Such a balance cannot be found in the energy proposal of his son G.W. Bush ten years later.

The 1992 National Energy Act served, for all purposes, as the energy plan of Bill Clinton's administration. When Clinton was elected, the country was in a recession and his immediate focus was on turning the economy around. The administration's most controversial effort linked to energy was a gasoline tax proposed as part of deficit reduction legislation. The administration's initial proposal was a tax of 10 cents per gallon to be devoted to deficit reduction.[5] The tax was widely condemned, particularly by the trucking industry. Fearing voter backlash from a higher tax, Congress eventually approved a tax increase of 4.5 cents a gallon. Truckers threatened a slowdown and predicted economic disaster as a result of higher prices linked to the tax. Two months later, the price of gasoline plunged to levels not seen since the late 1970s because of a glut of oil on the world market. Truckers fell silent and the tax protest fizzled out.

The Clinton administration devoted little attention to energy policy except to support the budget of the DOE, which funded grants to state energy offices and conservation programs. Energy policy fell off the national agenda as oil prices stabilized at relatively low levels and the economy began a sustained recovery after a recession in the early 1990s. By 2000, the budget deficit had disappeared and economists began to forecast budget surpluses for the next decade. Energy policy shifted to the states where electricity restructuring and deregulation was initiated in several states.

By the time George W. Bush took office in 2001, however, the national energy supply picture had changed significantly. The OPEC cartel had reorganized and was manipulating oil supply, raising the price of a barrel of oil on the world market to $35, the highest price since 1982. Gasoline prices in California rose to over $2 per gallon in the summer of 2000 and over $1.50 in the midwest and eastern states.[6] Natural gas prices also rose in the 2001 winter heating season because of supply shortages. Of greatest concern was the price of electricity in California, which had escalated to prices unheard of when utilities were regulated.

President Bush appointed his vice president, Dick Cheney, former CEO of Halliburton, Inc., an oil services company, to chair a task force to develop an energy policy to get the country out of what was declared to be an energy crisis. Bush had also been president of an oil company and had many political supporters in the energy industry throughout the country. One of his biggest supporters, the Enron Corporation of Texas, was also a leading supplier of wholesale electricity. The Cheney task force included many representatives of the business community and met in secret. Although the vice president claimed that the task force had consulted with environmental representatives, he later refused to release to Congress a list of names of all those consulted during the planning process.[7]

The energy strategy that emerged from the task force abandoned energy efficiency as a policy and instead proposed a massive program to increase the supply of all energy sources. Back on the table was drilling on the coastal plain of the Arctic National Wildlife Refuge (ANWR), which was projected to yield 600,000 barrels of oil per day by 2010. To increase electricity supply to meet growing demand, the task force estimated that the country would have to build 1,300 new generating plants over twenty years, some of them powered by nuclear energy. While the report did include a nod toward energy efficiency, Cheney in a nationally-televised speech described conservation as a "sign of personal virtue" but "not a sufficient basis for a sound, comprehensive energy policy" (*New York Times* 2001: 14). The administration promoted its strategy as the first national energy policy in twenty years.

While the task force was meeting to design the proposal, the price of electricity in California rose to astronomical levels. The state was forced to step into the market to buy electricity for the utilities, PG&E declared bankruptcy, and Southern California Edison was on the brink of financial collapse as well. Ratepayers faced price increases of 40 percent while the FERC refused to order price caps on wholesale electricity in the west. The EWGs, including Enron, Duke Energy, and Reliant, posted quarterly profits above 100 percent.

The Bush administration strategy was based on a presumed energy crisis linked to prices for natural gas, gasoline and electricity. By late spring, however, prices in all areas began to moderate and the crisis designation had less impetus for policymakers. After the September 11, 2001 terrorist attacks, the administration began to pursue energy policy more vigorously for national security reasons. Pressure was placed on the Senate to approve both the energy strategy and drilling in the ANWR. At this writing, no final action has been taken.

Energy policy at the national level had shifted emphasis from conservation (demand) to free market production (supply) during the Reagan Administration. George H.W. Bush retreated somewhat from this emphasis as he tried to develop consensus between the White House and Congress. His support of drilling in the ANWR was doubtless the result of his experience and pressure from his friends in the oil industry, but the Democrat-controlled Congress refused to go along with the plan. His son, who came into office with Republican majorities in both houses of Congress, made it one of his first proposals. By 2001, policy makers had grown comfortable with free-market economic theory and deregulation. The states too were moving toward deregulation lured by the promise of cheap electricity.

The California energy crisis, as we shall see, caused the states to reexamine their policy priorities. The recognition that states have other policy interests in electricity that go beyond the interests of the market caused many states to slow down in the rush to deregulate electricity. Before we look at electricity restructuring and the California case, it is useful to examine state policy interests and their historical development of energy policy since 1974.

3

The States and Energy Policy, 1975–1995

State electricity deregulation policy was designed to meet one goal: to reduce the price of electricity. Energy policy, however, is a complex of policy interests, the impacts of which vary by state.

This chapter looks at state energy policy over the period of 1975 to 1995, the year when states began to deregulate electricity. Key questions addressed here: What other policy interests are linked to states' energy policy? How have they changed over time? I provide a description of the evolution of state energy policy during the 1970s and the refocus on deregulation at the federal level during the 1980s as the Reagan administration eliminated federal support for state energy planning. The results of a study I conducted in the early 1990s reveal that states continued to develop energy policy in the 1980s to protect their complex energy policy interests against the uncertainties of the free market.

State Energy Policy Pre-1975

Prior to 1975, energy policy in the states was concerned primarily with regulation of electricity and natural gas utilities. The federal government had some regulatory powers over the interstate transmission of natural gas and electricity generation and sales because of its ownership of several power plants. The Tennessee Valley Authority was created by the federal government in the 1930s to provide electricity to rural towns in the south, and the Bonneville Power Administration was developed to market electricity generated from federal dams on the Columbia River. Although power generated by the federal government became a major source of electricity—25 percent by 1950—the private utilities continued to expand as new uses for electricity generated growing demand after World War II.

State energy policy at that time had two primary objectives. First, the public utility monopolies were regulated to ensure fair prices for customers and a reasonable return for the utilities. This system worked well, providing reliable supplies of electricity and natural gas at affordable costs, as well as steady dividends to utility companies' shareholders. Indeed, utility stocks were among the most reliable investments in those days and were a significant source of income for retirees throughout the country. Regulation also protected the utilities from having to pay the full costs of bad investment decisions, insofar as state public utility commissions would generally allow them to pass these costs along to ratepayers. This practice became one of the contentious issues of electricity deregulation in the 1990s.

A second goal of state energy policy was to promote the use of indigenous fuels to generate electricity. In some states—Kansas, Texas, and Oklahoma, for example—power plants burned natural gas and oil. In Ohio, Indiana, and Pennsylvania, on the other hand, coal was the primary fuel used for electricity generation. These energy-fuel industries also had significant political clout in their states to promote production and resist attempts to reduce the environmental impacts of fuel production and use that would impose higher costs on electricity production.

State regulatory power changed in the 1970s when the federal government assumed primacy over a number of policy areas. Beginning with the Clean Air Act Amendments of 1970, environmental protection and regulatory laws generally were structured to require state implementation of federal standards in policy areas that had previously been the jurisdiction of the states. During the early 1970s, a pattern of federal leadership in regulatory policy developed and states became the implementers of federal policy rather than developers of their own.

The 1970s saw a period of significant federal regulatory policy development in environmental management, consumer protection, and worker safety. The primary argument in favor of federal policy development was to establish uniform minimum standards for all states. This would ensure that all Americans had a uniform level of protection from hazards to their health and welfare. Moreover, federal standards created a level playing field for companies and industries that operated in different states. It, thus, overcame the problem of economic disadvantage for firms operating in different states with different regulatory schemes. It also reduced costs of production for companies operating in more than one state. For example, the automobile manufacturers supported the Clean Air Act's uniform standards requirement because it would spare them the costs of manufacturing different cars for different states.[1]

Second, many of these laws—the Clean Air Act, the Clean Water Act, the Occupational Safety and Health Act, the Consumer Product Safety Act, the Resource Conservation and Recovery Act, et alia—established standards that were designed to protect human health and, as such, could not be permitted to vary among the states. State standards were subject to political manipulation by companies that had economic power in the states. Companies not only lobbied against tough standards but also threatened to leave the state, taking jobs and tax revenue with them. This form of "economic blackmail" limited the ability of the states to establish standards to better protect the health of their residents. Federal primacy curtailed this problem to a great extent. By the middle of the decade, the states had become accustomed to federal leadership and even comfortable with it because it lifted some of the political burden that state legislators and governors had in imposing regulations on their in-state industries.

After the first energy "crisis" in 1973, the federal government began to take a primary role in developing comprehensive energy policy. During the Nixon and Ford administrations, the national emphasis was on independence from foreign oil producers. While there was policy activity to increase domestic supplies of oil and natural gas at that time, including construction of the Alaskan pipeline from Prudhoe Bay to Valdez, national policy also placed a major emphasis on energy conservation. Decreasing demand was seen as a viable means to increase supply in both the short and long terms. A simple maxim of the time was "a barrel of energy saved is cheaper than a new barrel." Moreover, in states that lacked an indigenous energy resource, conservation was their only means of managing supply and demand.

In the mid-1970s, Congress enacted two significant energy laws that provided guidance and funds to the states to develop their own energy policies: the Energy Policy and Conservation Act of 1975 and the Energy Conservation and Production Act of 1976. The first provided funding for states to establish state energy offices to promote energy conservation through public information campaigns. States were required to develop plans to reduce energy consumption throughout the state by

5 percent below the expected level of use without conservation. The second gave grants to states to implement energy conservation in public buildings, low-income housing, schools, and hospitals.

State Energy Policy Development in the 1970s

Federal energy policy shifted emphasis during this period from ensuring cheap and abundant supply to improving efficiency and protecting economic stability and national security.[2] In this new policy arena, the states and the federal government developed a partnership that depended on the states for implementation of many conservation and efficiency programs. Many of the states had much to gain from national policy that protected them from price shocks and uncertain supply. Other states profited from energy price hikes, so national policy, in effect, moderated the shift of state energy dollars from one state to another.

Henry Lee divides the states and their response to oil price shocks into four categories:

1. Those sixteen states highly dependent on oil: the New England states, the Mid-Atlantic states, Pennsylvania, Virginia, North Carolina, Florida, California and Hawaii.
2. States that relied heavily on natural gas and electricity and thus placed a greater emphasis on regulatory programs focused toward these two sources of energy.
3. Energy producing states, which already possessed a sophisticated government infrastructure to regulate and promote production.
4. Large agricultural or rural states in which allocation of supply remained an important issue, but energy programs aimed at policy issues were of less importance (Lee 1983:162).

The impact of energy policy on the states varies according to several factors. States that have no indigenous fossil fuel resources are energy importers and are vulnerable to supply shortages and price shocks. This is exacerbated where there are climate extremes that increase the need for reliable energy supplies and price stability. States in this category include Wisconsin and Minnesota, for example. These states are concerned about diversion of dollars away from the state economy to purchase energy. They have the greatest incentive to promote energy conservation and the development of renewable energy sources to improve their energy "trade deficit."

States that have abundant energy and natural resources, such as Texas, Alaska, and Indiana, on the other hand, may benefit economically from shortages and price increases. Energy producers in such states would tend to have political power and to oppose state efforts to develop conservation-based energy policies.

Two other factors that influence state energy planning are the environment and the economy. The environment is both a positive and negative influence. In states where environmental values are a high priority, low-pollution energy production and conservation will be favored. In states where pollution is high, energy policy is stimulated by environmental regulations. Energy conservation provides a positive linkage for these policy areas because reducing the consumption of energy also reduces pollution from its production.

Energy policy is directly related to the state economy in two ways. First, energy costs represent a major, controllable operating cost for industry and commercial businesses. Price hikes and shortages are disruptive. Second, economic development in the state is dependent on having an available supply of affordable energy. Maintaining an adequate supply of energy for all current and potential users is essential for states to support their economic base. States that have no indigenous energy resources have an incentive, therefore, to identify conservation opportunities and renewable energy sources. Alternative energy can also provide a new market for the state—ethanol fuels, for example, create an attractive market for agricultural states.

Energy prices have a significant impact on government operating costs. States and local governments, including schools, colleges, and other public entities, collectively have a lot of buildings, many of which are aging and poorly maintained. In addition, governments have a lot of vehicles—police cars, fire trucks, street sweepers, garbage trucks—most of which are high energy consumers. Energy costs in government operations, on average, are the second largest operating expense after personnel (Bailey 1984). Reducing government energy costs through conservation and efficiency can reduce spending pressure on public budgets. Indeed, an industry rule of thumb predicts savings of at least 10 percent from simple conservation measures such as weather-stripping and caulking doors and windows.

It is important to recognize the interactions of policy interests in the energy arena. Environmental protection remained a strong policy interest throughout the 1970s at all levels of government, so energy policy had to be designed to avoid significant impacts on environmental values. Air pollution controls required by the Clean Air Act of 1970 and its 1977 amendments raised the costs for electricity generation at the same time that energy fuel costs—oil, natural gas, and gasoline—were also rising. Consumers demanded lower prices for electricity and all other sources of energy, but these would hamper conservation incentives that work best with higher prices. The nuclear power industry was experiencing growing difficulty in siting new generators and rising costs due to greater regulation. The 1979 nuclear accident at the Three Mile Island power plant in Harrisburg, Pennsylvania, presaged the beginning of the end for nuclear power in the United States, at least for the next twenty years.

Given these complexities, it is not surprising that conservation and efficiency, or demand management, became the policy of choice for many state governments. Conservation is the cleanest and cheapest way to increase energy supply. It reduces operating costs for individuals, commercial businesses, large industrial users, and government at all levels. It also reduces demand for new generating plants and the pollution they emit. Finally, it protects state interests against price manipulation from outside the state borders. The last is a serious problem for states that are energy importers, such as Wisconsin and Minnesota.

Environmental and consumer activists in the 1970s also began to lobby for policies to promote the development of energy from renewable resources. Prior to 1973, policies to protect the five fuels displaced funding for research and development of electricity generation from renewables, principally solar power, including wind, geothermal, and biomass resources. Energy production was linked to fossil fuels, and there was no real concern for future supplies of these depletable resources. Government support of the nuclear power industry, beginning with the Atomic Energy Act of 1956, was supposed to lead to electricity generation that would be so cheap that meters would no longer be needed. There had been no similar support for the solar energy industry where technological and market developments were in their infancy in the 1970s.

Electric utilities had invested heavily in nuclear generating capacity by 1980, and, because of the decision policies of state regulatory agencies, they were able to pass along all the costs of this investment to ratepayers. This later became a considerable problem for deregulation efforts as these investments became "stranded costs" that had not been paid off. The full costs of nuclear power generation, including the cost of decommissioning the plants and disposing of nuclear waste, have never been incorporated into the pricing of electricity. Had companies been required to account for these costs, they might well have made more conservative investment decisions.

The energy crisis of the 1970s affected states differently. In states that did not have indigenous sources of energy supplies, energy policy development meant protection against the unfairness of the market. In these states, energy prices escalated and supplies dropped during the 1970s. Where heating costs became prohibitive, the elderly and poor were often forced to choose between food and utility bills. There were many cases of elderly people freezing to death in the northern states. Economic development was also threatened in energy-poor states that could not guarantee new businesses a reliable supply of energy at affordable prices.

Oil- and gas-producing states, on the other hand, enjoyed windfall revenue increases linked to energy production, especially after price controls on "new" oil and gas were lifted. These states were able to reduce taxes and invest in new public policy areas, including economic development. The move of companies from the Rust Belt to the Sun Belt during this period significantly changed the economies of states in both areas.

The sixteen states that were highly dependent on oil for heating and electricity generation were under political pressure to establish aggressive energy programs for different reasons (Lee 1983: 162). The northern states focused on increasing supply and reducing costs in order to protect residents and attempt to keep local industries. States in the Sun Belt, on the other hand, were experiencing rapid growth and needed energy policies to ensure reliable supplies for these new users and to foster more economic development.

Federal funding for energy programs helped the states to develop varying levels of expertise in energy policy and management during the 1970s. These programs supported the promotion of energy conservation, energy efficiency, and demand-side management. By the end of the decade the essential components of a stable national energy policy system were in place and there was a broad consensus across the country in support of energy efficiency and conservation. The results of these initiatives were variable across the states. Nonetheless, by the end of the

1970s, it was clear that "conservation had provided more new energy to the nation than any other source" (Kash and Rycroft 1984: 238).

The confluence of three policy interests—price stability and availability, economic development, and environmental protection—drove the development of state energy policies in the 1970s. With assistance from the federal government, in the form of both regulations and funding, states' energy policies at the end of the 1970s reflected the then-national consensus that efficiency and conservation should be the primary focus of U.S. energy policy.

Radical Policy Shift in the Reagan Administration

Everything changed after the 1980 election. Ronald Reagan's administration dismantled much of the energy policy infrastructure established during the Carter administration and turned energy over to the free market, shifting the policy emphasis from reducing demand to increasing supply. Funding for the state energy offices was phased out, as were individual tax incentives for conservation and solar energy technology. The Department of Energy (DOE) budget was shifted from supporting energy conservation and the development of synthetic fuels from coal and oil shale toward support of nuclear weapons development. During the 1980 campaign, Reagan had pledged to dismantle the DOE. Lacking the political support to do so, the administration used the budget process instead to change the agency's priorities.

Loss of federal funding, however, did not lead to wholesale closings of state energy offices or programs. Many states received new funds through "oil overcharge" allotments. Court decisions had held that the major oil companies had overcharged customers across the country during the 1970s. Multimillion-dollar fines were levied against the companies, to be paid out to the states over a multiyear period. In the absence of any feasible mechanism for returning the overcharges to individual customers, the funds were apportioned to the states according to population and gasoline consumption for the period. Most states received several million dollars each year from 1986 to 1993. Because the monies belonged to all taxpayers, oil overcharge funds were to be used for projects that had broad energy benefits. Many states used these funds to continue operating energy offices and to fund various energy management programs. A lot of oil overcharge money was used for weatherization projects for low-income property owners and energy assistance for the poor. In the 1980s, without energy policy leadership in Washington, states continued to fund their energy offices.

A new policy issue linked to energy production and use—global warming—appeared on the horizon in the 1980s. The response of the Reagan administration was to ignore the growing indications of global warming in the absence of what they considered to be strong scientific evidence. The signs increased throughout the decade—the discovery of an expanding hole in the ozone layer over Antarctica and a few record-breaking hot summers. Many reputable scientists began to express concern about the effect of human activities in altering the climate of the planet. Global warming, when it happens, will have different impacts on each state; the strongest effects, from a policy perspective, will be on energy demand and, ultimately, on economic development. States that presently have high heat loads will see the number of air-conditioning use days increase. Agricultural states may experience declining crop yields as high heat wilts crops no longer suited to the area climate. Increased demand for irrigation because of drought induced by heat waves will strain water resources as well as increase demand for electricity for pumping water.

State Energy Policy Development During the 1980s

State energy policy during the 1970s had been mandated by and largely funded by the federal government. James L. Regens has argued, however, that states alone could have developed energy policy. In 1979, he studied state policy responses to energy problems. He found that a number of energy policy measures had been implemented at the state level without federal mandates (Regens 1979). His analysis suggested, moreover, that public perceptions of the importance of energy as a problem were not significant in the development of state energy policy. He concluded that "the extent to which states choose to develop energy policy options appears to be primarily related to their structural composition, particularly their existing energy supply-demand system" (Regens 1979: 54). Regens postulated that the states could take a vigorous role in the energy policy process independent of the federal government.

In the early 1990s, I studied whether states had continued to develop energy policy during the period 1980–93, in the absence of federal leadership in this policy area. The aim of the project was to assess the extent to which the consensus on energy policy that developed during the 1970s

41

had been maintained in the states.[3] Seventeen Midwestern and western states were included in the study: Colorado, Idaho, Iowa, Illinois, Indiana, Kansas, Michigan, Minnesota, Missouri, Montana, Nebraska, North Dakota, Ohio, South Dakota, Utah, Wisconsin, and Wyoming. The research design used both quantitative data collection and case studies. General data were collected through a mail survey to state energy agencies. Case studies of selected states were developed through examination of published energy policy documents and personal interviews with individuals representing the executive branch, the legislature, and citizens groups in each state.

The survey instrument was designed to produce general information about (a) the existence and nature of energy policies in the states, (b) energy management initiatives taken by the state government, (c) regulatory and other barriers to improving energy efficiency, (d) potential impacts of energy policy on state industries, (e) transportation and environmental protection policies, and (f) awareness of potential global warming impacts on the state.

A comprehensive questionnaire was sent to the directors of state energy offices in each state. After repeat mailings, completed questionnaires were returned by twelve states: Colorado, Indiana, Iowa, Michigan, Minnesota, Missouri, Montana, North and South Dakota, Utah, Wisconsin, and Wyoming. While this sample is obviously limited, it is representative of the nation in that it includes states that have severe weather conditions in both winter and summer (Missouri, Kansas, North Dakota),[4] states that are energy producers (Colorado, Indiana, Kansas, Wyoming), and states that are energy importers (Minnesota, Wisconsin, Missouri). The findings from this study were compared with a study on energy management and conservation prepared by Frank Kreith and George Burmeister for the National Conference of State Legislators published in 1993.

Face-to-face interviews were conducted in seven states: Michigan, Indiana, Illinois, Minnesota, Missouri, Kansas, and Colorado. Telephone interviews were conducted in two additional states, Iowa and Wisconsin. The purpose of the interviews was to develop a set of state profiles to identify the political dynamics that influenced the development of energy policy. Face-to-face interviews were arranged with (a) the energy office, (b) a legislative staff member or legislator, and (c) an environmental organization in the seven states. These provided a triangulation of independent perspectives to address problems of bias and validity within the research design that could result from individual interviews.

Each interviewee was asked the same set of questions but the conversations were open-ended and heuristic. The questions focused on several factors: their personal experience with energy policy development and management in the jurisdiction, their personal feelings about the importance of energy policy for economic development and environmental protection, their perceptions about general public and political support for energy policy development, and their impressions about public awareness of global warming issues in the state.

In our sample, nine states reported that they either had a formal energy policy or were developing one: Indiana, Iowa, Kansas, Minnesota, Missouri, Montana, South Dakota, Utah, and Wyoming.[5] Wisconsin had developed a formal plan in 1986 at the request of Governor Tony Earle (State of Wisconsin 1986). Wisconsin is an energy-importing state and the plan emphasized conservation and the expanding use of indigenous energy fuels such as wood pulp and biomass for heating and electricity production. It also made recommendations for the use of anticipated oil overcharge funds to fund programs in local government operations and energy programs for low-income people. Earle, a Democrat, was defeated for reelection in 1986 by Tommy Thompson, a conservative Republican. The energy policy was discontinued, although many of its recommendations for oil overcharge funds were implemented.

Among those states that had energy plans, there was considerable consensus about the components. The primary components of state energy plans from 1991 to 1993:

- Subsidize heating costs/weatherization for the poor.
- Increase conservation by state and local government.
- Require utility companies to promote conservation.
- Develop energy management programs for state/local facilities.
- Develop awareness public relations campaigns.
- Revise construction codes.
- Develop energy standards for commercial buildings.
- Promote use of alternative fuels.
- Develop state-sponsored demonstration projects.

Several secondary components were identified by many states, indicating some agreement on the linkages between energy and other policy areas, namely, the environment and the economy. These included developing a comprehensive energy resource development plan; tax incentives for conservation by individuals and business; research grants to universities or business; tree planting programs; and increased mass transit.

What stimulated the development of these energy policies in the 1980s? The most critical energy problem identified in the survey was "lack of indigenous fuel supply," followed closely by "increasing costs due to federal regulations." Other problems cited included environmental concerns and radioactive waste. A few states indicated that excess power generation in the state served as a barrier to the development of energy policies because it provided no incentives for conservation.

States were asked to identify the priorities of their energy plans. These are shown below in order of importance (i.e., 1 = most important).

1. Increase conservation.
2. Save money.
3. Improve environmental quality.
4. Develop economy.
5. Use/market fuels indigenous to state.
6. Comply with mandates.
7. Reduce greenhouse gases.
8. Mitigate price shocks.
9. Increase supply

There are two points of interest in this list. First, increasing the supply of energy placed dead last as a priority of state energy policy. The states clearly saw conservation (reducing demand) and saving money on energy costs, linked with environmental quality and economic development, as their primary interests. Second, it was remarkable to find that reducing greenhouse gases placed in the ranking at all. There was considerable uncertainty at the time about global warming. The federal government, under both Reagan and Bush I, refused to develop global warming policy until they recognized a greater consensus within the scientific and industrial communities. Thus, it was noteworthy to find that global warming was of at least marginal concern to those states that developed energy policies in the 1980s. State energy officers identified several potential impacts for their states from global warming, including both positive and negative impacts on agricultural productivity, increased demand for electricity for cooling, and increased energy sales to other states. Their greatest concern focused on the state's environmental quality. One energy officer put it succinctly, "If the environment collapses, it's hard to run an economy."

The interviews revealed that in many states new federal legislation had stimulated interest in energy policy development. Three bills, in particular, led states to think about policies that would moderate the impacts of these regulations: The 1990 Clean Air Act Amendments, which included transportation funding sanctions for noncompliance with all air pollution standards; the Intermodal Surface Transportation Efficiency Act of 1991, which enhanced federal funding for transit and authorized $6 billion for transportation projects to help improve air quality in the states (Weingroff 2003); and the 1992 National Energy Policy Act (NEPACT). Thus, demand side-management, required by these laws, forced examination of conservation even in those states that enjoy energy surplus and where the electric utilities are powerful political players. To that extent, then, states could be seen as acting to defend themselves against federal regulation.

This study revealed two factors that are significant to the current study. First, the data showed that energy was no longer a single policy issue in the states. Whereas in the 1970s, energy policy was developed for its own sake, in 1990, it was seen to be linked with other policy interests, principally the environment and the economy. In the 1970s, states developed policies to meet the mandates of the federal government, even when such policies did not fit with state priorities. In the absence of federal mandates for energy policy in the 1980s, however, states developed energy plans that worked with regional needs and conditions while responding to federal regulations in other areas.

The study also revealed that the states' interests in this complex policy area were often in direct conflict with the promises of free-market theory to deliver cheap energy through competition. While the states ranked saving money as a priority, none reported that cheap energy prices were the way to do that. To the contrary, many energy managers expressed concern about falling prices as a disincentive for conservation. Cheap energy encourages overconsumption and stimulates demand for more energy supply. The states revealed clearly that their primary interests included environmental quality, economic development, and protection against price shocks. Increasing the supply of energy was the lowest priority because in most cases increasing supply can also lead to environmental degradation.

45

Although this study was completed in the early 1990s, electricity deregulation was not being discussed at the time this research was completed. Energy managers did favor private research, development, and marketing to improve energy conservation. The NEPACT had not been fully enacted when the data were being collected. None of the people I interviewed mentioned electricity deregulation as a possibility, including the chief lobbyist for the electricity industry in Indiana.[6] It is not apparent to me today that these state policymakers had any intentions of restructuring electricity in 1991. This implies to me that deregulation became a policy issue only after the establishment of electricity wholesale generators (EWGs) in the NEPACT. The development of EWGs made it possible to buy and sell electricity across state lines, something that would have been difficult before 1992. These new entities also became powerful lobbyists for the creation of new markets through restructuring.

What is very clear from this study is that states viewed energy policy as being coupled with economic welfare and environmental protection. These interests remained consistent over time from the beginnings of state energy policy development in the 1970s. In the early 1990s, many states recognized the negative effects of market uncertainties on their residents and businesses and were developing policies to overcome these effects.

Within a few years, however, electricity restructuring surged across the country, focusing state energy policy on one goal, reducing the price of electricity through competition and consumer choice. The consequences of this narrow focus were felt first in California, which ultimately reacted by stepping in to protect its other policy interests. Chapter 7 examines whether state energy policy interests have changed since 1992. The next three chapters look at electricity restructuring and the experiences of California and other states with deregulation.

4

Restructuring Electricity

An examination of the origins of the electricity industry reveals a strong relationship between the industry and government agencies aimed at encouraging the development of this new energy resource in a way that was productive for both the companies and the nation. Electricity became a viable commodity during the late nineteenth century during the same time that government regulation was born. Today we tend to forget that businesspeople supported government intervention in the market in those days, especially where it protected the interests of companies through limiting entry into the market and overcoming predatory market practices.

When creating a new industry, producers can incur high start-up costs and high risks of failure. Electricity generation requires large investments for the construction and operation of generating plants. A second major investment is incurred in constructing and maintaining the distribution system: poles, wires, and connectors to the final user. In the early years, companies saw clearly the advantages of a regulated marketplace to protect their investments from unbridled competition.

History of Electricity Regulation

The first power plant in the United States, the Pearl Street Station in Manhattan, owned by Thomas Edison, was opened in 1882. The industry was unregulated until 1907 when New York and Wisconsin established the institutions and rules by which utilities would conduct business in those states (Brennan et al. 1996: 21). In a typical political strategy of many industries of the time, "the privately owned electric utilities actively *sought* government protection from what Samuel Insull, one of the industry's founders, called 'debilitating competition' and to counteract growing municipal ownership" (Brennan et al. 1996: 21). Insull was Edison's protégé and owner of Chicago Edison, now Commonwealth Edison. He believed that electricity was a natural monopoly because the costs of competition in generation and delivery would be too high (Smeloff and Asmus 1997: 10).

In 1920, Congress created the Federal Power Commission as part of the Federal Water Power Act to regulate the prices of interstate sales of electric power and the field prices of natural gas, the prices charged by interstate natural gas pipeline companies (Joskow 1975: 17). The electricity industry grew rapidly; small private companies were eventually taken over by holding companies, reducing the number of firms providing electricity nationwide. In 1935, Congress enacted the Public Utility Holding Company Act (PUHCA), after investigations by the Securities and Exchange Commission (SEC) found evidence of stock manipulation.

Prior to the PUHCA, holding companies spanned several states and created complex corporate structures for generation, transmission, and distribution of electricity. The PUHCA was implemented by the SEC, which, over a ten-year period, created simple corporate vertical structures in which one company generates electricity, transmits it to local regions, and distributes it to the final customers (see Brennan et al. 1996: 23). Each company would operate within state borders with state regulation of their business operations. Transmission lines were interconnected across state lines, but there was little interstate transmission of electricity. Until the 1960s, utility companies were able to increase capacity fast enough to keep up with growing demand within their own states.

In 1965, a major power failure blacked out the northeastern United States from New Jersey to Canada. This led to the development of the North American Electric Reliability Council (NERC), established by the utility industry to better coordinate electricity transmission in cases of power failures. The NERC established ten regional councils that were responsible for maintaining the reliability of three transmission grids, the Eastern Intertie, the Western Intertie, and the Texas grid. These grids span the United States, Canada, and parts of Mexico (Brennan et al. 1996: 26), making it possible for states experiencing a shortfall in generating capacity to buy excess capacity off the transmission grid from utilities operating in another state. This was one of the important factors in restructuring the electricity industry forty years later. In August 2003, a much more extensive blackout occurred across the northeast from New York to Michigan and throughout Ontario. This blackout was caused by excess demand on the now-deregulated grid in a series of power grabs. See the Epilogue for a broader discussion of this event.

The underlying rationale for regulating the industry was that electricity generation, transmission, and distribution constitute natural monopolies. A natural monopoly exists when the costs of producing a product would be lower when one company provides it than when two or more firms compete for the market. Because the costs of electricity generation were high and economies of scale were necessary to maintain efficiency, electricity generation was considered to be a natural monopoly because competition could reduce prices below the cost of production. Transmission is arguably a true natural monopoly in that competition in transmission would require duplicate systems crisscrossing the landscape. In addition to the aesthetic problem this would present, the costs of constructing and maintaining such systems would be prohibitively high. Retail competition was likewise considered to be a natural monopoly so that multiple wires would not be strung along city streets and neighborhoods. The impetus to deregulate the industry came when one element of the vertical system—generation—began to be seen as a potential competitive market and no longer a natural monopoly.

Electricity is a unique commodity in many ways. Unlike natural gas, because it cannot be stored, companies must produce enough each day to meet the estimated demand. In a free market, producers will try to generate only enough electricity to meet anticipated demand so that there is not a surplus on the market that could drag prices down. Demand varies throughout the year according to weather and economic conditions in a state. Under regulation, power plants were built to a size that would meet peak demand, the highest demand anticipated during the year. As a result, a portion of the entire generating capacity of a utility company would be idle for most of the time, except during high demand periods, generally in the summer months when air conditioning is needed. According to Smeloff and Asmus, "the electric utility industry uses only about half of all the generating capacity that has been built in the United States. That means that fully staffed power plants are being paid for by captive ratepayers, yet remain idle for half the time" (Smeloff and Asmus 1997: 76).

Another feature of electricity that makes it different from other commodities is that once electrons are put into the grid, they are indistinguishable from all other electrons. In other words, the electricity purchased from Company A is mixed with that from Company B and the final customer cannot choose to buy only that electricity generated by Company A. In addition, customers cannot receive only those electrons produced by nonutility sources or generated from renewable sources like solar, biomass, or hydro. As discussed in chapter 2, the Public Utility Regulatory Policies Act (PURPA), enacted in 1978, required utilities to purchase electricity from nonutility sources or qualifying facilities (QFs) as an incentive for the utilities to increase the percentage of electricity generated from renewables in their mix. Taking the QF concept further, the 1992 Energy Policy Act (EPACT) created a class of exempt wholesale generators (EWGs) that can generate and/or sell electricity as wholesalers in competition with the utilities themselves. In a deregulated market, customers can choose to purchase renewable electricity by contracting with providers that put those electrons onto the grid.

Exempt wholesale generators are regulated by the Federal Energy Regulatory Commission (FERC), which is responsible for authorizing access to the utility's transmission grid if it is determined to be in the public interest. The FERC is legally obligated to ensure that EWGs are charging "just and reasonable" prices. It operates as an oversight agency in much the same way that the Securities and Exchange Commission regulates the stock market. Before deregulation, the FERC's mission was to prevent collusion and price fixing between EWGs and public utility companies. Since deregulation its primary role is to ensure against price gouging and market concentration that could constitute monopoly conditions. This role was seriously compromised during the California electricity crisis.

These developments in the EPACT are seen as the final pieces that made deregulation of electricity a real possibility. The industry had changed over two decades so that many of the conditions that made it a natural monopoly no longer existed. Prior to 1970, the big utilities were able to achieve economies of scale by building large generators and high-powered transmission lines. To sell their excess generating capacity and continue to increase profits, the utilities encouraged electricity consumption. Industrial customers received volume discounts; residential customers were advised by Reddy Kilowatt, a cartoon advertising character, that electricity was the biggest bargain in their family budgets.

In the early 1970s, growth in demand for electricity was about 7–8 percent per year. The number of power plants was doubling about every ten years. Many utilities planned to meet this demand with nuclear power plants. By the end of the 1970s, however, nuclear power had become exorbitantly expensive because of safety and environmental regulations, as well as the costs of construction and operations. The 1979 near melt-down at the Three Mile Island, Pennsylvania, nuclear plant effectively halted new construction of nuclear facilities in the United States. The remaining plants represented a huge expense for the utility companies that owned them, an investment that became a complicated policy issue during deregulation efforts.[1]

Electricity costs increased throughout the 1970s and demand growth dropped to about 2 percent per year (Smeloff and Asmus 1997: 17). Utility executives who had worried about a capital shortage for building new generators found instead that they had surplus capacity. New technologies for energy efficiency were developing along with environmentally benign power generation in the form of cogeneration and the use of renewable resources; the regulated utilities resisted their widespread adoption. For most companies, with big investments in expensive generating capacity, it was simply not in their best interest to encourage their customers to use less electricity. As mentioned earlier, Pacific Gas and Electric in northern California was one of the exceptions to this rule. The company was unable to meet growing demand for electricity in the 1970s and so developed a program of subsidies and incentives for conservation that saved the company billions of dollars in costs for new generating capacity.

Frustrated with the large utilities and their resistance to shifting away from fossil fuels or nuclear power to renewable sources of generating electricity, Congress enacted the requirement in PURPA that utilities buy electricity from private companies when that was a lower-cost alternative to building their own power plants (Smeloff and Asmus 1997: 18).

The most effective form of such electricity came from cogeneration, where waste heat from an industrial process is captured and used to turn turbines to generate electricity. Cogeneration plants that use combustion turbines (jet engines) had been shown to have efficiencies of 75 percent or higher. This compares with an efficiency of less than 50 percent for coal-generating plants. The new combustion turbine generators were small, could be built quickly, and better matched load growth (Smeloff and Asmus 1977: 19) so that the cost of electricity generation could be significantly lowered.

Electricity generation has heavy environmental impacts. The industry produces 72 percent of the nation's sulfur dioxide emissions and 36 percent of carbon dioxide emissions (Smeloff and Asmus 1997: 2). Sulfur dioxide from power plants in the Midwest is a primary component of acid rain and acid deposition in the northeastern states and southern Ontario. Transmission of emissions is a serious problem for areas that are downwind of the plants. In fact, if New York and New Jersey were to eliminate all in-state sources of sulfur dioxide, they still would not be in compliance with the Clean Air Act. Coal-burning power plants also emit large quantities of small particulates or dust that cause respiratory problems. Coal mining, especially surface or open-pit mining, also degrades land and water in areas surrounding the mines.

Nuclear power plants are often cited by the industry as being pollution free insofar as they do not produce the air and water pollution that coal plants do. They have their own set of problems, however. First, they generate nuclear waste that must be safely contained for thousands of years before it will finally reach a decontaminated state. At the present time, most spent nuclear fuel rods are stored in pools of water near the plants, some of them perched above or near major sources of fresh water like the Great Lakes or major estuaries, such as Chesapeake Bay.

Every material that touches the radioactive component becomes radioactive itself. Low-level radioactive waste, such as protective clothing, has to be stored safely away from environmental contact until it is deemed to be safe, often for hundreds of years. In addition, the nuclear power plants themselves have a limited life—twenty-five to thirty years—because of the degradation of materials exposed to radioactivity. This means that decommissioning old nuclear plants will also create large amounts of high-level radioactive waste that has to be disposed of safely. Contaminated buildings and structures have been exposed to varying levels of nuclear radiation. The U.S. government has been working for decades to solve the problem of nuclear waste disposal. It is an intractable problem that can have severe political consequences for state and local government leaders who cooperate to have nuclear waste stored in their jurisdictions.

Nuclear power plants are seen increasingly as a major hazard to the residents who live and work near them. Because of the increase in terrorist activity in the United States since September 11, 2001, nuclear power plants are seen as a potential target. Efforts to close the Indian Point nuclear power plant located in Buchanan, New York, approximately thirty miles north of New York City, gained momentum after the attack on the World Trade Center. This effort was strengthened by a state-commissioned report published in early 2003, which found that the evacuation plan for the area following a terrorist attack or an accident was seriously inadequate (Witherspoon 2003).

Nuclear power is often promoted as a cleaner fuel because it does not produce carbon dioxide (CO_2), a greenhouse gas that contributes to global warming. Fossil fuels burned for electricity generation are a major source of greenhouse gas emissions. All combustion in the presence of air creates carbon dioxide, our most plentiful greenhouse gas. Natural gas burns more completely than coal and generates less CO_2 per kilowatt hour, but the more electricity produced the more greenhouse gases are also generated.

There are other ways to generate electricity without adding carbon dioxide to the atmosphere: solar, hydroelectric, wind, and geothermal power. About 15 percent of electricity in California is already generated by hydro, wind, biomass and geothermal power (www.energy.ca.gov/electricity/generation_ownership.html), and the state is planning to increase that to 25 percent by 2020 (State of California 2003: 5). Sunshine in the western states makes solar power a viable option for individual generating facilities for both businesses and homeowners. In response to the 2001 crisis, the state developed a subsidy program for homeowners and commercial businesses to help cover the costs of installing rooftop photovoltaic cells (www.consumerenergycenter.org/rebate/index.php). During sunny days, these systems actually put electrons back onto the grid and buy electricity only at night or on very dark days.

Wind power is another significant source of renewable energy. A 1992 study of the Midwest by the Union of Concerned Scientists found that wind power in many states could be generated for less than 5 cents per kilowatt hour (Brower et al. 1993). At the time, retail prices for regulated electricity generated from fossil and nuclear fuels ranged from 4.83 cents per kilowatt hour for industrial customers to 8.21 cents for residential customers (Energy Information Administration/Annual Energy Review 2002: 25). California has several windmill generators and the potential for more. The state with the most potential wind resources is Kansas, which also has the largest known reserves of natural gas. Both are located in the western end of the state.

The 1992 act stressed greenhouse gas reduction as a component of national energy policy. First, utilities were required to do integrated resource planning to help them identify the costs of all options for adding peak load capacity, including new power plants, modifications of existing plants, purchasing power, energy efficiency and load management measures, improving transmission lines, and alternative rate structures (Smeloff and Asmus 1997: 52). Utilities were also required to develop demand-side management (DSM) programs where investments in conservation and energy efficiency could be shown to be as profitable as investments in additional electricity generation; and finally, they were encouraged to develop rate structures that would foster investments for efficiency in generation, transmission, and distribution of electricity.

Figure 4.1 shows investments in demand-side management programs in California from 1993 to 2000. It shows that utilities made significant investments in these programs to reduce peak demand until 1997 when the investments dropped off and continued to decline through the end of the decade. This coincides with the passage of deregulation legislation in California and other states.

The 1992 law also provided funding for state energy offices and cost-sharing grants to industry associations that were implemented through the Rebuild America program. In the 2003 Department of Energy budget, funding for nongrant state and community programs, presumably including the state energy departments, declined from $123 million in 2001 to $93 million in 2003 (U.S. Department of Energy). Rebuild America has been reorganized into the Weatherization and Intergovernmental Program (www.eere.energy.gov/weatherization.html) and funding was increased from $230 million in 2002 to $277.1 million in 2003 (U.S. Department of Energy).

The Road to Deregulation

By 1993, vertical integration of the electricity industry was becoming indefensible. The PURPA had opened the transmission lines to outside providers of electricity and the EPACT had authorized the formation of exempt wholesale generators to serve as brokers for the sale of electricity throughout the North American grid system. Several companies, including large public utilities, transformed their businesses in order to become participants in this new market.

The final piece of the deregulation puzzle was the technology revolution. With computers and integrated information systems, it was now possible for brokers to identify supplies of daily excess electricity anywhere in the market and to negotiate hourly prices to sell electrons to areas with a shortfall. It was now also possible to link buyers to sellers directly to enable them to find the lowest market rates. The old arguments

Figure 4.1 **Demand-side Management Expenditures for Electric and Natural Gas Programs**

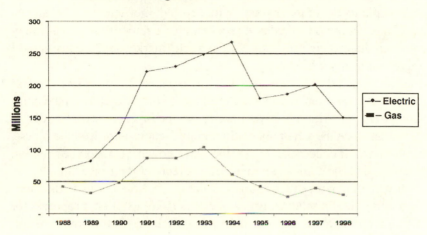

Source: California Energy Commission, Energy Commission, Publication No. P400-99-012, September 29, 1999, Figure 3, p. 6.

for having one company to produce, transmit, and sell electricity no longer persuaded. Nor was it necessary for consumers to be serviced only by companies within state borders.

Natural monopoly was declared to be dead as several states began to develop deregulation strategies. In April 1994, the California Public Utility Commission issued a proposal to deregulate electricity within four months in a bid to become the first state in the nation to enter this new world.

Issues in Electricity Restructuring

Deregulating electricity is not a simple matter. Several decisions have to be made about how consumers will interact with the electricity marketers and how electrons will be delivered over the jointly used, privately owned transmission grid. The principal issues that have to be addressed are whether competition should be at the wholesale or retail level (retail wheeling); how to market contracts between producers, marketers, and final customers; and whether utility shareholders should be reimbursed for so-called stranded costs.

Stranded costs may be utility investments that have not yet been amortized and/or long-term contracts that the utilities have entered into. Competition is supposed to bring down prices by opening the market to companies with the highest efficiency and lowest costs. If their prices are set to achieve a reasonable profit, then they will push the more expensive plants out of the market. In theory, old, inefficient coal-generating plants should be shut down as a result of competition because they cannot reduce their prices to the desirable market level. This should improve a utility's efficiency.

Most stranded costs are linked to investments in expensive nuclear plants that were approved by state regulators who also allowed the companies to increase rates to cover the costs of the investments. The utilities argue that since the state public utility commissions approved the investments and their concomitant rates, the states now have a moral obligation to ensure that the company's shareholders recover their investments.

How to deal with stranded costs is a major political issue in developing a deregulation scheme. Brennan et al. (1996) offer six proposals for stranded cost recovery: (1) contract renegotiation, (2) transmission surcharges, (3) compensatory exit fees, (4) accelerated depreciation, (5) auctioning off transmission facilities, and (6) making recovery dependent upon environmental improvements (Brennan et al. 1996: 105–7). In contract renegotiation, utilities would renegotiate contracts with wholesale customers to obtain compensation for stranded costs. Transmission surcharges require customers to pay an additional fee for use of the utility-owned transmission system, until stranded costs have been recovered. Exit fees would be paid on top of the surcharge by those customers who buy electricity from other suppliers, thus contributing to the problem of stranded costs. Accelerated depreciation would simply allow companies to increase the capital recovery allowance used to compute rates. Utilities might also be allowed to auction off their transmission lines on the premise that the funds would be used to cover stranded costs. Another proposal would require utilities to bring existing plants into compliance with new source performance standards of the Clean Air Act in order to be eligible to recover stranded costs.

Each of these proposals has strengths and weaknesses. The fundamental question of whether utilities should be treated any differently than other businesses that suffer stranded costs is difficult to address. On the one hand, utilities made investments in expensive generating plants with the assurance that they would be able to recover their costs because they served a captive regulated market. Thus, they made decisions that might not be made in a competitive market where there is uncertainty about investment recovery. On the other hand, regulators generally approved rate increases so long as they were based on fair recovery of investments with limited profits. The companies had no incentive to develop low-cost alternatives for generating power so long as regulators set prices on a "cost plus" basis. Their shareholders were promised a steady return on their investments. There was, in a sense, a covenant between the regulators, the companies, and the shareholders. California policymakers approved a transition surcharge for a three-year period or until the stranded costs for each utility were amortized. In exchange, the utilities agreed to a price cap and an across-the-board 10 percent discount for all customers.

There are precedents for stranded cost recovery during the regulatory era. Two utilities, Long Island Lighting Company in New York and American Electric Power in Ohio, were allowed to recover from ratepayers the costs of converting nuclear power plants to coal-burning plants prior to completion of the construction. In both cases, the companies had invested huge sums in these plants—the Shoreham plant in New York and the Zimmer plant near Cincinnati, Ohio—only to have construction and operating costs escalate dramatically. The Shoreham plant was ultimately doomed because of safety concerns about a nuclear generator located in a densely populated area. The Zimmer plant was deemed to be simply too expensive to operate. Both states' regulators approved rate increases to pay for what amounted to bad business decisions. After the Three Mile Island accident, Consolidated Edison was permitted to place a surcharge on electricity rates to partially compensate shareholders for the costs of the accident.

These examples also demonstrate the partnership that existed between the states and electricity utility companies during the regulatory era. Electricity is a vital product in the economy of the United States. In a regulated market, the privately held utilities are critical links to maintaining the standard of living to which Americans have grown accustomed. Regulators thus were obligated to ensure the fiscal health of these companies because the states could not afford to lose their product. This same scenario was played out in a different way during the California crisis, which will be discussed in the next chapter.

Retail wheeling refers to the ability of individual customers to buy electricity directly from any provider who "wheels" it onto the transmission grid. The biggest concern with retail wheeling is that if the large industrial users buy power directly, then other consumers—small businesses and residential consumers who cannot negotiate with providers directly—will become captive customers of the utilities and their higher priced product. Because utilities would still own the transmission systems, they could add charges for transmission of electricity from outside sources that would raise customer prices and diminish the advantage of direct contracts. The only way to avoid this would be for individual suppliers to build their own transmission systems, a prohibitively expensive proposition as well as environmentally and aesthetically negative.

The alternative to retail wheeling is expanded wholesale competition. In this variation, only the generation segment of the industry is deregulated. Generators use the wholesale market and utilities distribute electricity to final customers. Local distributors keep their monopoly franchises for selling electricity to retail customers and continue to be regulated by the states. Customers can choose to purchase electricity from any wholesaler but are connected to the grid through the regulated utility. Integrated utilities are required to divest their generators from the distribution system. This is the mechanism that was chosen in California. The utilities were required to sell off most of their generating facilities. Customers would choose a provider who delivered electricity through the utility's lines and retail distribution system.

There are two principal marketing methods for electricity services: bilateral contracting and a pooling mechanism known at the time as a "poolco." Bilateral contracting refers to transactions between two parties under specific supply contracts—generators and distributors, marketers, or final customers. A poolco is operated by a coordinator that provides for short-term power transactions through a centralized spot market.

In bilateral contracting, generating companies make contracts with local distribution companies who pay the generators for the electricity. An independent system operator (ISO) is responsible for balancing the supply and demand of electricity on the transmission grid. Distribution companies deliver power to the customers' premises and receive payment for the service (Brennan et al. 1996: 45).

The ISO can also enter into contracts with generating companies or large users to change their supply or usage according to the demands on the system. In periods of shortage, large users agree to cut back demand in return for favorable transmission rates. Likewise, in periods of excess supply, generation companies make themselves available for shutoff. Because electricity cannot be stored, there is nowhere for excess electrons to go. Some kind of balancing mechanism is essential.

The poolco model can have the coordinating responsibilities of the ISO and also the operation of a centralized spot market for electricity. It serves as a wholesale broker, soliciting bids from generators regarding the prices and amounts of power they are willing to sell during each hourly segment of the following day. Its proponents believe that it is the only way to make sure that electricity is provided at the lowest price. Long-term contracts were considered undesirable because a generating company might operate a high-cost generator under a contract at a time when a lower-cost generator owned by another company is idle. Spot markets encourage the generating companies to resell low-cost electricity during those periods rather than produce their own higher-cost electricity (Brennan et al. 1996: 56). Thus, spot markets would, in theory, produce the lowest-priced electricity with the highest market efficiency.

On the other hand, a poolco might also create market power rather than facilitating true competition. "A highly concentrated generation market increases the chance that generators would collude to manipulate the spot price—that is, they could limit the amount of power sold in the market in order to raise the price and thus their profits" (Brennan et al. 1996: 58). And the poolco itself could become a market power. "If the poolco is the sole gatekeeper to participation in an electricity market, it could exercise market power—charging high rates to power distributors and offering low prices to generators—as if it were a monopoly seller and monopsony buyer" (Brennan et al. 1996: 58).

Another concern about deregulation was the loss of investments in demand-side management and energy efficiency. In a free market of electricity buyers and sellers, no provider would have reason to promote efficiency. This is true even for companies that provide electricity generated by "green" energy sources. In order to get enough customers to demonstrate that there is a demand for green electricity, the companies have to sell as much electricity as they can.[2] Thus, they are in the ironic position of encouraging consumption and increasing demand while advocating environmental protection at the same time.

Social Costs of Electricity Generation

Generating electricity has some significant social costs. It is questionable whether these can be dealt with fairly in a deregulated marketplace. The two most important costs are social equity and environmental protection. Electricity is not an ordinary commodity that consumers can choose or not choose to buy depending on price. It is a necessity of modern life the absence of which can cause severe hardship. One rationale for state regulation was to manage the price of electricity so that it was not out of the reach of low-income citizens. Deregulation, or market-based electricity, was advocated to the states as the only way to achieve the lowest possible market prices. Regulated utilities were assumed to be inefficient and over priced solely because they were monopolies.

The experience in California illustrates, however, that market prices go in two directions. When prices spike as they did, the impacts are harsher on the poorer and more vulnerable citizens. In the past, utilities were required to provide low-priced services to low-income citizens. The federal government subsidized power systems and rural electrification programs that brought electricity to farms and sparsely populated areas. Companies in a competitive market have no reason to provide for social equity. Their primary responsibility is to their shareholders and not to the community. Indeed, most of them are not even located within range of the community if the market system works as it is supposed to.

In addition, electricity generation and transmission have a heavy impact on the environment. The negative externalities associated with electricity are air pollution, including sulfur emissions and fly ash (soot); water pollution, including the discharge of heavy metals and hot water into lakes, rivers, and estuaries; nuclear waste; potential health effects from electromagnetic fields; and greenhouse gas emissions, primarily carbon dioxide and nitrogen oxides. Acid deposition/rain from coal-burning plants falls in areas far distant from the sources. Transmission lines are unsightly and environmentally intrusive. Their location may present an environmental justice problem as well if they are located in low-income or rural neighborhoods. Coal mining for electricity production leaves scars on the land and contaminates water as well as damaging the health of its workers.

Since the 1970s, several environmental protection laws, as well as the Occupational Safety and Health Act, have tried to reduce the environmental impacts of electricity production. The industry lobbied against these laws, but under regulation they were held to an expectation to protect the public interest as well as the industry's. In a deregulated market, however, the emphasis is on producing electricity at the lowest cost. Many economists have argued that competition should encourage the use of more efficient, low-cost power plants (Brennan et al. 1996: 115). It is also true, however, that one way for companies to reduce costs is to shift the cost of externalities like pollution onto the public. The Bush II energy proposal argues for exactly that by emphasizing the need to relax environmental regulations in order to build more power plants.

The loss of incentives for integrated resource planning and demand-side management counts among the greatest social costs of deregulation. Individual companies making individual decisions will opt for building plants at their lowest costs. For the near term that probably means using some form of fossil fuel, most likely natural gas. Even though the 2001 Cheney Task Force recommended increasing nuclear power generation, the social and political problems related to its use and disposal are still formidable. The costs for construction and operation are many times greater than the costs of natural gas or coal-burning generating facilities. Safe disposal of radioactive wastes has not yet been developed. The heightened fear of terrorist attacks on these plants since September 11, 2001, also makes it unlikely that nuclear power will become more widespread in the near future.

Without some form of government coordination, the market is not likely to produce a mix of fossil, renewable, and efficiency methods that can come close to that designed through integrated resource planning.

Conclusion

This chapter has provided an overview of the history of electricity regulation and the major events that led to deregulation and restructuring of the industry. By 2001, most states had considered deregulating and several had implemented it. California was the first state to implement deregulation. The legislation was enacted in 1995 and the market was opened to consumers in 1998. The next chapter provides a case study of deregulation in California: how the features of the legislation were developed, how it worked in practice, and an analysis of what went wrong. Reverberations from the California electricity crisis have been felt around the country since the summer of 2001. The case study serves as a tale of caution for governments learning how to operate in the market.

5

Restructuring the California Electricity Market

A Case Study

In July 2000, San Diego Gas and Electric Company (SDG&E) tripled electricity rates. A year earlier, the company had recovered all of its stranded costs[1] and the California Public Utility Commission (CPUC) had authorized the utility to begin charging market rates. Because the company was buying electricity on the spot market at the hottest time of the year when demand for electricity is highest, it was paying the highest price per megawatt that the market would bear. Wholesale prices soared and SDG&E passed the costs along to its customers.

Not surprisingly, consumers were outraged. Deregulation had been heralded as the way to *lower* prices; now consumers were paying significantly more for electricity each month than they had under regulation. Through the summer, a series of power emergencies and localized blackouts occurred all over the state. In August, the CPUC approved a rate stabilization plan for SDG&E customers to cap household rates at $68 per month, retroactive to June 1, 2000, and extending through December 31, 2001. Legislation enacting this plan extended the cap through 2002.

The crisis seemed to be contained—until November 2000 when Pacific Gas & Electric (PG&E) in northern California and Southern California Edison (SCE), the other major independently owned utilities (IOUs), suddenly faced drastically increased prices for megawatts purchased on the short-term wholesale market. Over the next three months, retail electricity prices jumped from 8 cents per kilowatt-hour to as much as 35 cents. The utilities were still prohibited from passing the full costs of electricity along to ratepayers because they had not yet recovered all their stranded costs. Under the terms of the state's deregulation policy, they were also required to give all residential customers, including those who contracted with another provider, a ten-percent reduction on electricity charges. The IOUs retained the responsibility for transmission and distribution of electricity, regardless of customer choice of provider, and were required to refund to customers the difference between the rates charged by alternate providers and the price-capped electricity delivered by the IOUs. The scene was set for a financial disaster.

By the end of the month it was clear that the state was facing a crisis of unknown proportions. In early December, the utilities asked consumers to save power during peak daylight hours by waiting until 8 P.M. to turn on their Christmas lights. The Independent System Operator (ISO), the entity responsible for coordinating electricity transmission, issued its first-ever Stage Three alert on December 7. A Stage Three alert is ordered when the state has less than 1.5 percent of its electricity reserve. Stage Three alerts enable the ISO to increase the power supply by requesting voluntary reductions from large users. The ISO can also order rolling blackouts as the need occurs.

Just after Christmas, the price of natural gas in the state jumped to four times the prior-year price. This further increased the price of electricity generated by natural gas—about 50 percent of supply.[2] This put more pressure on PG&E's cash flow because the company could not pass these new costs on to retail customers. Suppliers became reluctant to contract with the company because they were uncertain that they would be paid.

In January, the CPUC approved a price increase of 1 cent per kilowatt-hour for PG&E and SCE customers. This failed to shore up the utilities' financial condition, however, and both Moody's Investors Service and Standard and Poor's downgraded the companies' credit ratings to one level above junk bond ratings, effectively curtailing their ability to borrow money to buy electricity on the open market. On January 10, PG&E asked the state for help in buying natural gas, arguing that it did not have enough cash coming in to pay its bills. By the middle of the month, the company's credit rating had been further downgraded to low junk status and it was in default on bank loans and credit lines. Electricity suppliers refused to continue selling to the utilities.

Finally, on January 17, the ISO ordered statewide rolling blackouts. Governor Gray Davis declared a state of emergency and authorized the state Department of Water Resources to enter into contracts directly with electricity suppliers. The state was desperate to develop a longer-term solution to this crisis, which was exacerbating the economic decline and increasing costs of operations for government as well as business and residents. On February 1, the California legislature approved legislation allowing the state to negotiate long-term contracts with energy suppliers and to sell up to $10 billion of revenue bonds to buy power.

The Federal Energy Regulatory Commission (FERC), which is responsible for ensuring that wholesale prices of electricity are "just and reasonable," refused to order price caps for the western states. Curtis Hebert, chairman at the time and a protégé of then-Senate majority leader Trent Lott, argued that the problem was one of supply and demand that the market would overcome if left to operate freely. Newly elected President George W. Bush, a Texas oilman with close ties to Enron CEO Kenneth Lay and other energy industry executives, refused to intercede despite the pleas of governors from California, Washington, and Oregon.

As the crisis worsened throughout the winter, the price tag grew by millions each month and rolling blackouts continued throughout the state. Eventually, the independent electricity providers abandoned the retail market and returned their customers to PG&E and SCE. The state initiated discussions to buy the transmission networks of the two utilities as a way to improve the companies' cash balances. Pacific Gas and Electric filed for bankruptcy protection before signing the agreement. Just before filing for bankruptcy, however, PG&E awarded $50 million in bonuses and raises to 6,000 senior managers and employees. SCE agreed to provide low-cost power for ten years in exchange for the state purchasing its transmission lines for $2.7 billion.

The governor delivered a statewide televised address, urging residents to conserve electricity. Legislation was quickly enacted to supplement existing programs for low- income assistance and energy efficiency and to develop several new programs. Pacific Gas and Electric and the state Energy Commission restored incentives for demand-side management, which had been developed prior to deregulation. These included rebates to consumers for purchase of compact fluorescent light bulbs, installation of photovoltaic roof panels, and the replacement of older appliances, especially refrigerators.

The state ultimately negotiated a contract to purchase electricity over ten years at a price of $138 per megawatt (Gaudette 2001). The agreement was based on prices on the spot market at the time of negotiations, long-term prices, and estimated demand per month assuming normal weather conditions and continued demand at historical levels. Even with the contracts, there were predictions of rolling blackouts throughout the summer, in anticipation of normal demand for air conditioning. In June, a heat wave brought record high temperatures—as much as 20 degrees above normal in northern California—but no blackouts. Californians had taken seriously the need for conservation and had reduced their electricity use by as much as 20 percent.

By this time, the federal government had begun to send signals to the market that helped to bring prices under control. In May, the FERC, under new chairman Patrick Wood, a former utility commissioner from Texas, finally imposed a price cap on wholesale prices in the western states after refusing to do so all winter on the premise that the free market would work best to solve the problem and price caps would only drive suppliers out of the market. In contrast to these predictions, price caps stabilized the market and suppliers continued to offer their product at prices below the caps. By the end of June, wholesale electricity was selling for $100 per megawatt down from $750 per megawatt the year before.

Then in July, the heat wave dissipated and record low daily temperatures were posted. Demand plummeted. The state, which had contracted to buy 30,000 megawatts per day at $138 per megawatt, was forced to sell as much as twenty percent of it back to the market at much lower prices. The price for these excess megawatts was around $25 each and some critics accused the state of selling its electricity for as low as $1 per megawatt (Gaudette 2001: 1).

Electricity Restructuring in California

What caused this experience in the first state to restructure its electricity industry? Many voices blamed the state's deregulation policy itself for the problems. Consumer groups argued that it was a state giveaway to big business and the utilities. Energy companies and some economists asserted that the state did not go far enough in deregulating the electricity market. The state had only partially deregulated, they said, by capping retail prices while opening up the wholesale market. The biggest criticism was that prices skyrocketed because the utilities were prohibited from entering into long-term contracts and instead were required to purchase electricity on the volatile spot market.

To determine the validity of these criticisms, it is helpful to understand how deregulation was developed in California, what the aims of the policy were, and why these policies, which look so foolish in hindsight, were adopted.

The original proposal to deregulate electricity in California was developed by Daniel Fessler, then-chairman of the CPUC. Fessler admired the efforts of British Prime Minister John Major to deregulate electricity in Britain. In addition, the CPUC believed that California electricity rates were too high and that competition in the free market was the only way to bring them down. In April 1994, Fessler proposed that deregulation be ordered in four months, with written comments on the proposal due in only thirty days and no scheduled public hearings. Then-Governor Pete Wilson, also a free market conservative, enthusiastically supported this proposal to make California the first state in the United States to open electricity to competition.

The controversial proposal immediately drew strong criticism from several quarters—the utilities, environmentalists, consumer groups, and small business. It was strongly supported by the California Large Energy Consumers Association, which had lobbied for its members to have the ability to buy electricity directly from suppliers in neighboring states more cheaply than from the state's utilities. There were also veiled threats that large users would move out of the state if they could not obtain lower electricity rates through the market.

The final plan was not signed into law until 1996. Direct purchasing, or retail wheeling, was eliminated in favor of a wholesale power pool—a poolco called the Power Exchange (PX)—which would set the prices that would be paid for bulk power on the spot market. A nonprofit Independent System Operator would coordinate and schedule the delivery of electricity over the transmission system. The energy wholesaler Enron lobbied to ensure that the PX would be separate from the ISO (Lazarus 2001). The Power Exchange would be monitored by the Federal Energy Regulatory Commission as it has authority over wholesale power sales under the Federal Power Act.

The utilities would retain ownership of their own transmission systems but were required to sell most of their generating plants. This was intended to prevent them from exercising monopoly power in the transmission and distribution of electricity. The companies sold their generating facilities to other companies outside the state, such as Duke Energy in North Carolina and Reliant Energy in Texas. Pacific Gas and Electric also set up a holding company so that it could compete as an energy marketer in the new restructured market. While the retail company was going bankrupt during the 2001 crisis, the parent holding company was posting record profits.

It is important to understand how strongly policymakers and power experts at the time believed that the free market would bring down prices of electricity dramatically. Simple economic theory assumes that sellers will reduce prices in order to gain a greater share of the market when buyers are able to choose from several providers. In the mid-1990s, when the proposed policy was being debated, there was a surplus of power in the western states. California utilities were already buying power from neighboring states to meet peak demand. It was assumed that this surplus would continue and that it would keep prices low after deregulation. It was also assumed that companies would rush to build generating plants to meet growing demand and that competition alone would increase electricity supply. Moreover, because the companies could buy electricity at wholesale prices from anywhere on the continent, it was also believed that they would seek out the lowest prices available.

The independently owned utilities were originally opposed to deregulation. Their biggest concern was their ability to pay off their stranded costs if forced to reduce prices or lose customers in the face of competition. These costs were linked to past investments in nuclear power facilities that the CPUC had approved under regulation. The companies argued that because they made these investments to benefit all ratepayers, their shareholders alone should not be left with the costs.

At the same time, policymakers feared the potential market power of the utilities. Three large companies dominated electricity generation and distribution in California. After deregulation, these companies would be forced to carry other companies' electrons on their transmission lines and distribute them to the utilities' former customers. A very real concern was that the utilities would crowd out other companies and load up transmission systems with their own electricity. To control any remnants of monopoly power and to offer the possibility of maximum consumer choice in electricity provider, the legislation required the utilities to sell many of their generation facilities. The companies were left with the most expensive plants, including unamortized nuclear generators, which could not be sold. To offset these costs, legislators eventually approved a surcharge, the Competition Transition Charge, which utilities could charge retail customers for five years or until their investments in these stranded assets had been completely amortized, if sooner. The utilities also retained ownership of the transmission and distribution systems. Electricity would be delivered to customers in the same way as before but the service provider would be optional. The IOUs were required to continue serving customers that did not choose a direct service provider.

Pacific Gas and Electric split into two companies—a holding company, PG&E Corporation, that was able to compete as an exempt wholesale generator (EWG) and Pacific Gas and Electric Company to handle retail distribution. Another subsidiary, PG&E National Energy Group, owns thirty power plants in ten states with others under development or construction. From 1997 to 1999, Pacific Gas & Electric Company transferred $4.1 billion in generating assets to the parent company and its subsidiaries (Oppel and Holson 2001: A17). During the spring 2001 crisis in California, the retail company declared bankruptcy while the parent company and subsidiaries posted record profits.

To encourage the utilities to reduce their costs, the CPUC approved a price cap, setting the maximum price that the utility could charge. The price cap was used as a performance-based ratemaking device. Under this concept, companies would be encouraged to buy electricity at prices below the cap and would be allowed to keep any balance left over after sales as profit. Thus, the price cap was a free-market device to encourage efficient operation. It also served as a floor to protect the utilities from predatory market pricing, so the companies were guaranteed this price no matter how low the market price might be. This ultimately became the mechanism that drove the companies into bankruptcy. Like the price ceilings on oil in the 1970s (see chapter 2), the price caps on electricity were designed to be a floor below which prices could not fall. In the midst of the crisis, the floor became a ceiling instead that drove the California companies to bankruptcy.

The legislation also required the utilities to give all residential customers a 10 percent rate reduction whether or not they purchased their electricity from an alternative provider. The price cap and rate reduction were designed to protect residential and commercial customers and to show immediate savings from deregulation.

All of the legislation was based on the belief that the free market would bring greatly reduced prices and abundant supply to meet the needs of the growing California market. That is the way it is supposed to happen according to every Economics 101 textbook. What went wrong? Was California a case of market failure, political failure, or, in reality, a grand market success?

Explaining the Crisis

As we examine the situation in the winter of 2001, several questions come to mind. To begin with, what caused the sudden increase in prices in the winter, a time of normally low demand? A number of causes were suggested by experts, economists, and pundits. It was asserted that excessive demand had developed in the five years since deregulation coupled with the absence of construction of new generating facilities in the state since 1990. The surplus of electricity in 1995 at the start of deregulation had become a deficit by 2000 as the demand for power to run dot-coms and Internet server farms had grown in the state's hot economy. Second, the state's strict environmental protection laws were said to be a deterrent to building new plants, making the approval process too lengthy. During 2000 alone, environmentalists and local politicians had quashed at least three proposed new power plants in northern California.

Many blamed the state's "flawed" restructuring plan that deregulated the wholesale market but continued to regulate the retail market. Enron Corporation's CEO Kenneth Lay asserted that the state really needed *more deregulation* and not a return to "inefficient regulation" (Lay 2001). By requiring the IOUs to purchase wholesale electricity on the volatile spot market instead of through long-term contracts, the critics said, the state had only partially deregulated the market, and, as a consequence, jeopardized the financial health of the utility companies and ultimately the state government itself. According to this argument, moreover, had the utilities been able to pass the higher wholesale costs along to retail customers, the balance between supply and demand would have been reached more quickly as customers reduced their demand thus freeing up more supply.

The loudest voices at the time blamed California consumers, who, it was alleged, had drastically increased their consumption of electricity. The stereotypical Californians were depicted as sitting in their hot tubs sipping wine while their computers, lights, and gadgets ran 24/7, with no concern for the amount of electricity they were using. What was mysterious to most residents and policymakers, however, was how suddenly this "excess demand" had appeared. Until November 2000, there had been no public warnings from the companies or the government about demand outpacing supply.[3] Indeed Californians, like people all over the country, had been encouraged to consume because of the roaring economy and to keep it roaring. Furthermore, deregulation advocates had promised that the market would rush in to meet any demand—customers could buy electricity from companies anywhere in the country at low prices. Was there an electricity shortage elsewhere in the country that would explain this supply-demand imbalance that was driving prices up so precipitously in California?

At the time, there was a shortage of electricity in Oregon and Washington because of a drought that had reduced the generating capacity of hydroelectric facilities. This was one factor that constrained supply in the regional market at the time. I know of no reports of electricity shortages in other parts of the country that winter. Moreover, by spring, companies in Washington State and British Columbia had learned how to manipulate their supply in order to take advantage of the lucrative California market. Bonneville Power Company, owned by the federal government, paid farmers $330 for every acre that they did not farm so that irrigation water they had contracted for could be used to generate electricity to sell to California at $375 to $400 per megawatt on the spot market (Harden 2001: A18). Companies in British Columbia and the Los Angeles Water and Power Department, a municipally owned plant, also moved to provide electricity at these attractive high prices.

One factor that significantly limited in-state supply in California from November to March was the closure of three major generators for maintenance, removing as much as 15,000 megawatts of electricity from the market. Winter is traditionally a time of lower demand, so most maintenance is performed during this period. These were plants that the utilities had been forced to sell. Under utility ownership of these plants, such maintenance closures were staggered in order to ensure sufficient generating capacity throughout the period. Historically, according to statistics kept by the California Independent System Operator, less than 3,000 megawatts at a time would be off-line because of plant maintenance. In December 1999, 2,569 megawatts were off-line compared with 8,988 megawatts in December 2000. This imbalance continued throughout the winter of 2001. In April 2001, a total of 14,911 megawatts were off-line compared with 3,329 the previous April.[4] The fact that so much capacity was down at the same time raised eyebrows among state leaders and citizens and increased suspicion that manipulation of in-state supply was related to a larger industry scheme to hike prices.

In addition, excess demand did not play the role alleged by the state's detractors. It turns out that Californians are far from the energy hogs they are depicted to be. Indeed, California ranked forty-sixth among the states in energy use per capita in 2000 thanks in part to the IOUs demand-side management programs over the fifteen years leading up to deregulation in 1996 (Energy Information Administration, State Energy Data 2000). Neighboring states of Nevada, Oregon, Washington and New Mexico ranked higher. Texas was ranked sixth in energy use per capita. While there was some demand growth in California during the last half of the 1990s, population growth in the neighboring states increased demand there at a faster rate. Because California had been importing excess electricity from these states, their demand growth thus reduced the amount of excess capacity that had been in place before California deregulated its market.

Nor was the supply picture as drastic as had been depicted. The governor dedicated several new generating facilities in the late spring and summer of 2001, plants that had been in development before the crisis. In early 2001, the state embarked on a fast-track plan to build power plants. Environmental rules were softened and the approval process was shortened in order to bring as much power on-line as quickly as possible. By May, plant maintenance had been completed returning 15,000 megawatts to the market. The new capacity in June and July helped to increase the supply available within the state.

The other factors that helped the state avoid blackouts after June were conservation and weather. Californians know how to conserve energy; they have been doing so for twenty years. In an address on April 5, 2001, Governor Gray Davis asked residents to take strong conservation measures to lessen the threat of summer blackouts. It was predicted at that time that the state would face a series of rolling blackouts over the summer because of normal peak demand. Emergency legislation was enacted that provided $1 billion to supplement existing energy efficiency programs and create new programs. The IOUs offered residents a discount if they reduced their usage by 15 percent over the previous summer. The state developed a subsidy program for residential and commercial installation of solar roof panels to self-generate electricity. Commercial lighting was dimmed, hot tubs were turned off.

The blackouts never happened. To be sure, the summer weather was unusually cool except for one heat wave in June, but there is no doubt that conservation made the difference (see Krugman 2001). Peak demand in June was 14.1 percent lower than in June 2000, a reduction of 5,570 megawatts (Gornstein 2001). Even during the June heat wave, demand never approached the limits of available supply.

In response to the judgment that deregulation policy itself was at fault, the state began to develop the institutional capability to participate directly in the market. The state Department of Water Resources (DWR) was authorized in January 2001 to contract directly with power suppliers, after they had refused to sell to the utilities because of fears of nonpayment. The DWR eventually obligated $12.5 billion from the state general fund, effectively wiping out the state's budget surplus at the time. The state requested approval from the CPUC to issue a bond in that amount to repay the state coffers.

On May 16, 2001, the governor signed legislation to create the California Consumer Power and Conservation Financing Authority as a means of getting the state more actively involved in the electricity planning and development business. The authority was given broad powers to issue $5 billion in bonds to buy, lease or build generating plants. Of these funds, $1 billion was earmarked for conservation programs. The governor appointed S. David Freeman to head the authority. Freeman has a long history in the energy business, having led both the Tennessee Valley Authority and the Los Angeles Department of Water and Power. He was coordinator of energy policy in the administrations of Lyndon Johnson, Richard Nixon, and Jimmy Carter. The new agency was designed to protect the interests of consumers by providing enough generating capacity to avoid future shortages in the retail market. It is to emphasize energy conservation and efficiency as means to increase supply and to focus on integrated resource planning for energy development, thus reinstating programs that were eliminated during restructuring.

By the end of August, the crisis was sufficiently mitigated that there were no longer any fears of rolling blackouts in the state. Many problems lingered on, most notably the state's efforts to reach an agreement with Southern California Edison to purchase their transmission lines.

The experiment in deregulation seemed to be at an end as the state developed its own capability to manage the market and assumed a far more prominent role in electricity production than it had under regulation. The CPUC suspended consumer choice—direct access to power providers—in order to guarantee the state enough customers to pay for its long-term contracts. It also granted the DWR the authority to increase rates as needed if prices increased because of fuel price hikes. Many of the DWR contracts had been negotiated with suppliers that use natural gas for power generation. The price of gas was expected to rise because of increasing demand forcing up the price of electricity as a result.

Questions lingered about the behavior of the EWGs during the height of the crisis. The state petitioned the FERC to investigate price gouging by the companies and claimed that California had been overcharged by as much as $9 billion. In the spring, evidence began to emerge that companies had acted deliberately to withhold electricity from the market to drive prices up. A year later, documents from the failed Enron Corporation outlined several strategies that the company used to manipulate the market and drive up prices (Kahn 2002).

El Paso Natural Gas Company was found to have manipulated the supply of natural gas into the state that also increased the price of electricity. The FERC analysts reported evidence that El Paso along with Enron and other companies had manipulated natural gas prices in California. California imports 85 percent of the gas it consumes and the state has a shortage of gas pipelines into and within the state (Oppel 2001: A1). El Paso was found guilty in September 2002 of illegally withholding natural gas from the state in order to drive up prices. The chief administrative law judge of the FERC, Curtis L. Wagner Jr., found that the company's pipeline used only 79 percent of its capacity and that "half of that unused capacity was caused by several factors including a failure to operate the pipeline at a high enough pressure and nonessential maintenance that could have been done at other times" (Oppel and Bergman 2002: C2). In March 2003, the company agreed to a $1.7 billion settlement with the state of California, and implicated Sempra Energy as a coconspirator. Sempra is the parent company of Southern California Gas Company and San Diego Gas and Electric (Douglass 2003: C2).

The Aftermath

By September, the crisis had passed. The state experienced no blackouts, new electricity generating plants were either operating or under construction, and conservation programs continued to encourage consumers to reduce demand. Prices continued to fall, as the economy moved toward recession following the terrorist attacks of September 11, 2001. By November electricity was trading for as little as $19 per megawatt and the state was seeking to renegotiate its contracts.[5]

Deregulation itself became one of the victims of the California crisis. The CPUC approved eliminating consumer choice in September 2001 and returned all retail customers to the IOUs to ensure that they would be able to recoup their debts. The state was still attempting to take control of the transmission system. Ironically, the failed experiment in deregulation, designed to free the industry from government intervention, resulted in greater government control over the marketplace.

Governmental entities began to develop plans for self-generation of electricity. Having learned the lesson of the importance of having control over supply, municipalities across the state began to consider developing municipal utility districts (MUDs) to generate their own electricity. The powerful examples of Sacramento, Los Angeles and Alameda, where MUDs had protected their residents from the crisis, served as momentum for these studies. When the original deregulation legislation was enacted, municipally owned utilities had successfully lobbied for exemption from deregulation. The Los Angeles Department of Water and Power and the Sacramento Municipal Utility District were designated as energy providers and eligible to trade on the state power grid. Their customers were not eligible for the mandated 10 percent rate reduction, as a result (Kraul 1996). Throughout the crisis, however, the companies were able to provide their customers with electricity at stable prices and sold excess electricity to the grid at the height of the crisis, thus reducing their costs of operation.

East Bay MUD, the water district in Alameda County to the east of San Francisco Bay, held public meetings in the spring of 2002 to discuss branching out into the electricity business. In November 2001, voters in San Francisco narrowly defeated a ballot initiative that would have authorized the city to take over PG&E by eminent domain and operate it as an MUD. The city of Hayward began a study to determine if the city should become an exempt wholesale generator. The city would be able to buy wholesale electricity from a proposed generating facility to be built in the city or from any electricity supplier and sell it at retail to its residents.

Individual citizens also moved to protect themselves from another crisis brought on by market extremes, whether normal or manipulated. Sales of solar electricity systems continued to increase, helped by the state's 50 percent rebate program. Gains in electricity supply due to conservation continued in part because of state programs, but also because many residents had made permanent reductions in usage through the purchase of new energy-efficient lighting fixtures and appliances.

Market theory was perhaps the biggest victim of all. None of the sweeping promises of the champions of deregulation were realized. Prices did not come down; suppliers did not rush in to serve consumer choice. A regulated system that most ordinary citizens thought worked well enough had been abandoned in favor of a wild and volatile free market that served the interests of a few large companies at the expense of small businesses and retail users in the state. There seemed to be lots of losers in the state and only a few winners—most prominent of which were the energy-trading companies that had lobbied aggressively for the plan in the first place. Many Californians tend to be skeptical about big business in the best of circumstances. Thus, this market failure for the state and market success for the companies became a major political failure as well. Some part of deregulation may remain—the ISO, for example—but major components of the plan are likely gone forever.

Deregulation's grand vision fell so short of meeting the state's other energy policy interests that it is unlikely that any California politician would risk supporting a return to the free market any time soon. This may be the ultimate penalty for the free marketeers who so skillfully used the market to their own advantage without consideration for the policy and political interests of the people of California.

6

Restructuring in Other States

While California blacked out in the winter of 2001, other states deregulated electricity seemingly without a hitch. Pennsylvania, for instance,
attracted ninety-six start-up companies when full retail choice went into
effect on January 1, 2001. Discounted electricity rates due to deregulation resulted in savings of up to 20 percent over the next year. By May
of 2002, however, 27 percent of the startups had dropped out of the
market and 44 percent of their customers had returned to the big utilities. The savings also dropped to 2 percent compared with the utility
charges (Lowe 2002).

Other states that began deregulation after California, such as Texas,
Ohio, and New York, did not experience the same troubles. They were
able to attract other providers and offer their consumers choice. Electricity supply remained sufficient to meet demand without the price
shocks Californians experienced.

Why was deregulation apparently so much more successful in other
states than in California? Was it simply that the California policy was
fundamentally flawed? Did other states have smarter policymakers who
were able to build better protections into their policies? Are there significant differences in these states' deregulation policies? Or were they
just lucky that California was first and therefore the sacrificial lamb for
market abuses?

Deregulation Policies in Other States

All state deregulation policies contain roughly the same features: a time-
table for implementing retail choice; requirements for utilities to give
other providers access to utility-owned transmission lines; amortization
of stranded assets; and restructuring of the major independently owned

77

utilities (IOUs). A fundamental question for all states is how to contain the market power of the IOUs. In California and many other states, the IOUs were required to sell their generating facilities but continue to operate the transmission and retail distribution systems as regulated monopolies. The IOUs could then form other entities to compete as energy providers with start-up companies and other energy providers.

In Pennsylvania, the IOUs were not required to divest their assets and continued to control about 80 percent of electricity production in the state (Lowe 2002). Start-up companies bought electricity from the IOUs. When the IOUs raised wholesale rates because of increased fuel costs, the new companies were forced to raise their own rates. The IOUs thus retained significant market power in the deregulated market. An additional constraint in the Pennsylvania market is the reserve requirement for all providers imposed by the PJM Interconnection, the independent system operator for Pennsylvania and New Jersey. Each provider is required to have a reserve of electricity capacity for emergencies. This rule was probably enacted in the wake of the 1967 East Coast blackout. In the deregulated market, it penalizes providers that do not own their own power plants because they must buy reserve capacity from the IOUs but not resell it. This raises their business costs while providing no benefit to them. Relaxing or eliminating the reserve requirement would reduce these costs and improve the market in ordinary times. It is wise to remember, however, that regulation is about protecting the interests of consumers, not the market. Having no reserve when an emergency strikes will result in the same kind of price spikes seen in California when the supply dropped.

When states require their IOUs to sell their operating facilities, the purchasers are often a new subsidiary of the existing IOU (Pacific Gas and Electric) or a subsidiary of an IOU in another state (Cinergy, Duke Energy). The major difference in operations of these plants is that they are no longer subject to many of the regulations that they were under the IOU's ownership. This restructuring led to one of the critical factors in the California crisis when several plants in the state were shut down for maintenance at the same time. The number of megawatts off-line was triple what had been the practice under regulation. Without a coordinator each company planned closures independently, resulting in a major shortage at the time of year when there is normally a surplus.

Pennsylvania had some major advantages over California. It began deregulation with a surplus of generation supply in 1999 and the transmission system that allowed for easy access to the grid across the Mid-Atlantic states. It also benefited from a plethora of retail providers that came into the market. While Pennsylvania had ninety-six competitors, California consumers had fewer than five. Virginia was unable to attract outside providers because the price there was already relatively low (www. americanhistory.si.edu/csr/powering/past). Without a competitive price to offer, new providers will not enter the market, and consumers will have little incentive to switch providers. Another roadblock to building a competitive market where prices are already low is that companies will be drawn to states only where they can charge higher prices and make higher profits. The companies themselves have little incentive to enter a market in a state where prices are already low.

Texas began full deregulation on January 1, 2002. Six months later, only 4 percent of ratepayers had switched to alternative providers. Some regions of the state were exempt from retail choice because of the absence of a regional transmission system in those areas. Texas required its utilities to divest 85 percent of their generating capacity. The state, home of the Enron Corporation, was not immune to the problems that plagued California. An Enron affiliate, New Power Holdings, folded in the spring of 2002, after booking almost a third of all switches during deregulation (Piller 2002). Enron was also fined by the Texas PUC for using phony "wash trades" to drive up prices and revenues (Piller 2002). Wash trades, also known as round-trip transactions, are sham transactions in which a company sells a product and buys it back. This inflates the company's sales figures. The PUC also acted to prevent companies from creating congestion on the grid and driving up prices artificially.

Ohio's deregulation program also began on January 1, 2001. At the time, the Ohio PUC had certified thirty-eight energy suppliers; by the end of 2002, only two remained in the market (Tongren 2003). Ohio's law permits municipalities to establish an opt-out community aggregation buying group. These groups negotiate with providers to obtain low prices for their members. Consumers can opt out of these groups and choose their own provider. The Ohio Consumers' Counsel (OCC) found that by the end of 2002, about 98 percent of Ohio's residential customers had switched through a group and that suppliers were not marketing directly to individual customers (Tongren 2003). The OCC also found that there was very little competition in large areas of the state.

If provider choice was the rationale for deregulation, it does not appear to be working very well. In all states that have deregulated, the original number of competitors has declined considerably over time.

Some states—California and Virginia, for example—attracted few competitors in the first place. A study by the National Center for Appropriate Technology, published in September 2002, reported that few companies were willing to serve residential customers. "In Ohio, Massachusetts, and New York, there are either no marketers or only one or two marketers offering competitive electric service to residential customers in most utility service territories" (Foster Electric Report 2002).

The study examined electricity deregulation in Ohio, Massachusetts, Texas, and part of New York, and natural gas deregulation in Georgia. It found that residential customers, particularly low- and middle-income residents, were generally worse off after deregulation, especially if they were subject to short-term price pass-throughs. Low-income residents are more prone to be charged higher prices because they can be switched to a provider of last resort that has no competitors. The exceptions were found in Ohio and Massachusetts where customers are involved in opt-out aggregation. Because these buying groups are coordinated by a political jurisdiction, all residents enjoy the benefits unless they opt out. The poor or the less clever negotiator is not disadvantaged in the marketplace in these cases.

The California energy crisis spurred a number of delays in the deregulation plans of some states, and in one case, Nevada, the governor reversed deregulation legislation altogether. The justification for the delays was primarily to allow states time to study the state electric transmission systems and the generating capacity to support competition, that is, to build power generating plants if needed. These states are apprehensive about deregulation after watching California's experience. Here are some examples of how the California energy crisis prompted other states to react:

- The governor of Kentucky called a previously unscheduled Energy Policy Board meeting, in order to discuss whether that state is at risk for power shortages similar to those in California, and whether the state power grid can handle the new power plants slated for development.
- Montana delayed the transition period toward deregulation to the year 2007, while simultaneously providing low-interest loans for new or upgraded transmission facilities or generation plants.
- Oregon's governor called on residents, businesses, and local governments to reduce usage in order to conserve.

- West Virginia placed its deregulation plans on hold until a study could be conducted to differentiate the situation in California and that state, as well as to conduct a study on tax law changes needed before deregulation takes hold. In addition, West Virginia's electricity program offers lighting grants for schools, nonprofits, hospitals, and local governments. In February 2003, the Energy Information Administration described restructuring in West Virginia as inactive (Energy Information Administration 2003).
- Minnesota decided not to undertake deregulation because of energy supply shortages in the region.
- Nevada's governor issued the Nevada Energy Protection Plan that spells out a strategy to both protect consumers from skyrocketing prices and develop power plant transmission line construction (www.eia.doe.gov/cneaf/electricity/chg_str/nevada.html).

In New York, where deregulation went into effect in June 2001, cities and entrepreneurs began to develop alternative energy sources, such as fuel cells to generate electricity for homes, along with demand-side management (Johnson 2001). The electricity surplus that existed in 1996, when the legislation was enacted, was supposed to last until 2005. Instead supplies tightened and prices rose by forty percent between 1999 and 2001 (Banerjee and Perez-Pena 2001).

Choice and the Market

Consumer choice is one of the primary purposes of deregulation. Without choice, there is no competition and without competition, prices can only go up, or so basic economic theory assumes. Choice/competition was supposed to lower electricity prices after deregulation. Yet most states that deregulated also required a certain reduction in prices during a transition period so that residents were not subject immediately to the volatility of market prices. Considering the objections that consumers raise when gasoline prices fluctuate in response to seasonal demand and world market conditions, it is not hard to see why policymakers wanted to cushion these effects for an initial period.

Yet choice is not forthcoming in many states that have deregulated. All states have seen the number of providers shrink while some states have not been able to attract many providers in the first place. Prices that fell initially have risen in all states with deregulation, as fuel price hikes are passed through to consumers. Along with price uncertainty, consumers also face supply uncertainty, as states no longer regulate planning for new capacity.

Given these uncertainties, it is not surprising that fewer than half the states have active deregulation plans as of July 2003. Figure 6.1 shows the status of deregulation in the states. No new deregulation policies have been enacted in the past two years.

The electricity market is now a hodgepodge of regulated and deregulated companies with the deregulated companies amassing greater political power to pressure states to deregulate. The FERC has proposed national policy to require deregulation to make the market uniform. This might make sense from an industry perspective, but not from a public policy perspective in individual states.

What Compels States to Deregulate?

Rhode Island's State Energy Office Web site offers a glimpse into the high hopes that the state legislature had when it enacted deregulation legislation in 1996:

> The legislature finds and declares the following: (1) that lower retail electricity rates would promote the state's economy and the health and general welfare of the citizens of Rhode Island; (2) that current research and experience indicate that greater competition in the electricity industry would result in a decrease in electricity prices over time; (3) that greater competition in the electricity industry would stimulate economic growth (www.rilin.state.ri.us/PublicLaws/law96316.htm).

The reality for Rhode Island's deregulation did not match these expectations. In fact, consumers have paid higher electricity costs, due to increased fuel price hikes, and there are few alternatives for people wanting different power generators than what was originally offered under regulation. Of the small number of customers who chose alternative providers, most quickly returned to IOUs (Rhode Island Public Utilities Commission 2001).

The impetus to deregulate came originally from the 1992 National Energy Policy Act and, more specifically, from the efforts of Kenneth Lay, CEO of the Enron Corporation, to develop exempt wholesale generator status in that law. Lay then embarked on a major lobbying effort

Figure 6.1 **Status of State Electric Industry Restructuring Activity**
(as of February 2003)

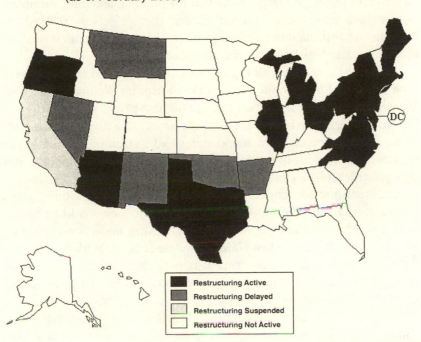

Source: U.S. Department of Energy Web site; available at: www.eia.doe.gov/
cneaf/electricity/chg_str/regmap.html.

to get deregulation policies enacted into law in individual states. Then-
Governor Bush (Texas) phoned then-Governor Ridge (Pennsylvania) to
put in a good word for Kenny-boy (Bush's nickname for Lay).

The other thrust toward deregulation came from economists and conservative think tanks that favor privatization over government management.
Their message has consistently been that regulation keeps prices up and
deregulation will automatically bring prices down through competition.

The first states to adopt deregulation were, in fact, those states that
have long had high electricity prices. They had strong pressure from
large electricity users (industrial and large commercial facilities) to allow them to contract with electricity providers other than the regulated
utilities. Residential customers and small businesses stood to gain much
less from deregulation—because they use relatively little electricity compared to big users, their potential savings individually are proportionately

small. Their political support was needed to get the legislation enacted, however, so states generally sweetened the pot by mandating minimum price reductions at the initiation of choice. Except in New York where the plan was instituted through gubernatorial fiat, deregulation was approved by state legislators for the governor's signature.

Note that the states with high prices also appear to be states with high demand, for example, New York, California, Pennsylvania, and Massachusetts. Hawaii, which has the highest prices in the nation, is unable to deregulate because it cannot connect to a transmission grid. Thus, the high price/high demand states had a strong incentive to deregulate. States with low prices and low demand have generally not deregulated, and Virginia's experience illustrates that it is hard to attract competition when prices are low to begin with. On the other hand, those states can become exporters of electricity to their wealthier neighbors and enrich the state coffers without taxing their own residents. This was the situation when California deregulated. With its high demand and high prices, California was persuaded by large users and other businesses that unless the state deregulated so that prices could come down, the companies would move across the border to Arizona, Nevada, or Oregon. Federal energy policy law would ultimately make it possible for these companies to contract directly with lower-priced providers in any case. Because there was a surplus of electricity in the western states when the policy was developed, California policymakers and consumers expected prices in neighboring states to remain low and even to go down more after deregulation. By the time deregulation began in 1998, however, demand in California and neighboring states had risen. Population growth in Nevada and Arizona drove up demand in those states. Drought in Oregon and Washington further limited the supply of electricity in the winter of 2001. When California's prices rose, those providers diverted electricity from their own customers to capture higher profits from California, driving up prices in their own states as well.

Why Do Electricity Prices Vary from State to State?

Three factors principally account for most of the difference. First, states with thriving economies and/or population growth will have high demand for electricity, and in-state supply does not keep pace with it. Energy demand correlates positively with economic growth.

A second factor is the fuel used to generate electricity. Prices in Washington and Oregon have been historically low because hydro plants are used to generate much of their electricity. So long as there is normal rainfall in the Pacific Northwest, the "fuel" will be abundant. Fossil fuels like coal, on the other hand, are more expensive to use primarily because of environmental regulations. Natural gas is becoming the fuel of choice for newer-generation electricity plants, but this fuel is also subject to price fluctuations. A sudden increase in the price of natural gas in December 2000 contributed to the price shocks in California. Nuclear power plants also drive up prices. These plants are one of the principal reasons that the utilities demanded recovery of their "stranded assets" in return for their political support for deregulation.

Third, states that have stringent environmental protection laws will have higher prices. These regulations cover the siting and construction of power plants as well as pollution control for burning fossil fuels. States with strong environmental protection laws—California, Pennsylvania, and New York, for example—have higher electricity prices than states with less stringent laws—Arizona, New Mexico, and Texas, for example.

With regulation, states maintained a balance between supply and demand for industrial use, economic development, and residential/commercial purposes. Those states where environmental protection is a strong public policy value also managed the trade-offs between generating capacity and the environment. Under deregulation, however, states are pressured to loosen environmental regulations in order to streamline the approval process for construction of new power plants. This was particularly the case during the California crisis. The state was berated for not having approved construction of new power plants during the 1990s. In response, the state weakened environmental protection and sped up the review process so that more capacity could be built in the state quickly. Once the economy cooled off, however, few of those plants were actually built, leaving the state vulnerable to future supply shortages when the economy recovers.

Deregulation may also push prices up in lower price states that abut high-price states. Prices rose in Oregon, Washington, and British Columbia during the winter of 2001, partly because of the general drought conditions, which reduced electricity supply, but also because the companies reduced in-state supply further by selling to California at greatly inflated prices. In any market, companies will act to maximize their own profits with little concern for the effect on consumers. With no legal constraints on predatory market behavior, companies will behave exactly the way they did in the western market during the winter of 2001.

How Much Can or Will Prices Fall When Demand Drops?

In theory, prices should come down when demand drops because of either increased supply or economic decline. The promise of deregulation was lower prices because of increased competition and supply. The reality is somewhat different, however, as the states are learning. Most of the new competitors in the electricity market are not producers who would build new capacity. They are only traders, middlemen who buy electricity from a provider and auction it off to states through their independent system operators. In general, supply is not increasing, only the number of sellers, and prices are not falling with decreased demand. In California and New York, retail prices rose after deregulation, offset slightly by mandated reductions in the deregulation legislation. In Pennsylvania and New Jersey, savings virtually disappeared less than two years after deregulation (Lowe 2002). Montana suspended deregulation when prices rose precipitously.

How Much Can Prices Fall?

Economic theory promises that competition—many producers—can automatically bring prices down because of the supply-demand dynamic. In a market where start-up and operating costs are high, however, how far can prices fall? Because new plants are expensive, producers in a free market will not invest in new capacity during a slow economy. They prefer, logically, to maintain supply at the current level so that prices can be maintained at the level needed to cover their costs of construction and operations. Without a guaranteed price, they stand to experience significant losses by building new capacity that would drive prices down. From their perspective, an increase in demand above current capacity is preferable. From the states' perspective, however, an increase in supply with declining prices is preferable to meet peak demand needs and attract economic development. Without the kind of market management available under regulation, states no longer have the ability to plan electricity supply and demand or to moderate prices across all customers.

Who Really Benefits from Deregulation?

In theory, everyone benefits in a deregulated market where users have a choice among many suppliers. In electricity restructuring, it appears that most of the benefits so far have gone to the energy companies themselves, including energy traders, companies that did not exist before deregulation. Many of the old-line utilities created a separate energy-trading company, especially those that were forced to sell their generating assets. Large electricity users also benefit because they can contract directly with energy providers and lock in favorable rates through long-term contracts.

Overall, choice for retail customers has declined everywhere that deregulation has been implemented and prices have not maintained low rates over time. In some states, there never was much choice. Pennsylvania and Ohio initially had a large number of new energy companies competing for retail customers. Those numbers have fallen within a relatively short period of time as the start-ups have fallen victim to rising costs of electricity from the same utilities that they are competing against.

Studies of deregulation are finding that promised savings have not materialized outside of those mandated by legislation, most of which are in effect only until stranded assets are paid off. Consequently, we could conclude in summer 2003 that residential and small commercial customers were no better off than they were under regulation, and some were worse off. A study of Massachusetts, Texas, Ohio, and part of New York by the National Center for Appropriate Technology found that choice and lower prices were achieved only through the use of opt-out aggregation (Foster Electric Report 2002). In this strategy, municipalities or other branches of government aggregate all users within their jurisdiction and negotiate with providers for the best prices for the group. Individual customers can notify the government if they want to opt out of the group. Only Ohio and Massachusetts use this strategy so far. Such buying groups were not legal during regulation. So, ironically, local governments in these states have assumed a stronger role in determining the price of electricity than they could have without deregulation.

While the experiences of other states with electricity restructuring have not been as catastrophic as California's, they do not appear to provide a strong argument to persuade other states that have yet to implement deregulation. The risk of another California market crisis is probably small because the backlash against the companies has been so damaging to them. Whether other states are willing to take this risk remains to be seen. Deregulation activity has come to a halt for the time being and the weak economy has also eased the demand for electricity. The memory of Enron's manipulations is still fresh, and California is still trying to recoup $9 billion in overcharges from the winter of 2001. In June 2003, the FERC ruled that contracts negotiated during the height of the crises were valid (Federal Energy Regulatory Commission 2003). California was thus denied authority to renegotiate the contracts despite above-market costs. States are dealing with large budget deficits that require major spending cuts or tax increases. Policymakers may feel that the political price that they would pay to restructure electricity in their state may simply be too high at this time.

In chapter 7, we look at what the states reported as their energy policy interests in the late 1990s, after the beginning of deregulation, in comparison with my 1992 study.

7

State Energy Policy in 2001

In the summer of 2001, the Mission Statement of the California Energy Commission read as follows:

> It is the California Energy Commission's mission to assess, advocate and act through public/private partnerships to improve energy systems that promote a strong economy and a healthy environment.
>
> It is the vision of the California Energy Commission for Californians to have energy choices that are affordable, reliable, diverse, safe and environmentally acceptable. (www.energy.ca.gov/commission/mission_statement.html)

These statements illustrate succinctly the interests that the state of California holds for its energy policy. Despite the rush to turn electricity over to the free market, the state's energy policy interests appear to remain the same as they were a decade earlier before restructuring began.

The 1992 study outlined in chapter 3 reveals that the states' energy policy interests are inextricably linked to policies for the poor, the economy, and the environment.[1] These findings are consistent with studies conducted in the late 1970s. Electricity restructuring creates an energy policy that is linked primarily to market interests. The advocates for market-based energy policy imply that prices will fall so low that the poor will have no difficulty paying and the economy will thrive as well. Impacts on the environment are dealt with through the choice option. In a market, people who value the environment will show their preferences by choosing to pay a higher price for electricity generated from "green" sources. And because there is no longer any requirement for the state to produce its own supply of electricity, environmental values in the state can be protected by buying electricity from sources outside the state.

The reality of the California experience of 2000–2001 differed markedly from this theory. In the aftermath of the experiment, all consumers were paying much higher electricity rates than they were before deregulation, the economy was flagging,[2] and the state approved construction of new power plants all over the state, relaxing environmental standards to speed up construction. The mission of the State Energy Commission, however, continues to represent the energy policy goals of the majority of Californians and the state's policy interests.

This chapter examines the energy policy interests of the states since deregulation began to spread across the country. The research for this chapter sought to document the states' energy policy interests ten years after the study described in chapter 3. Visiting the web sites of all fifty states, we identified the missions and programs of their energy offices. State Web sites were identified using links from the Web site of the National Association of State Energy Offices (www.naseo.org/members/states.htm). Information was gathered on the following factors:

- the location of the state energy office within the state government structure;
- the mission of the state energy office, if provided;
- the primary programs of the state energy office, as stated on the Web site; and
- any programs specifically related to electricity.

As the primary sources for this research are Web-based, the results may not reveal the entire range of activities of the state energy offices. While the majority of the Web sites are fairly detailed, others are less so. This point aside, the results do provide a useful framework for discussing state energy office activities circa 2001. Definite patterns and trends were detected in all of the focus areas.

State Energy Offices

State energy offices were initially established in the 1970s with funding from the federal government. When that funding disappeared in the 1980s, many states continued to fund the offices using allocations from court decisions on oil overcharges in the 1970s. In the first Bush administration, the passage of the National Energy Policy Act of 1992 mandated the establishment of state energy offices and restored federal funding to support them.

Location of State Energy Offices in the State Government Organization Structure

The location of the energy office is a clue to the state's energy policy priorities. All state energy offices are supposed to promote energy efficiency and demand side management. The major purpose of these programs—for example, economic development or environmental protection—varies among the states.

Twenty-two state energy offices are located in a type of Department of Economic and Community Affairs (Alabama, Alaska, Florida, Illinois, Maine, Michigan, North Dakota, and Tennessee); Economic Development (Arkansas, Hawaii, Massachusetts, Mississippi, Nevada, Ohio, South Dakota, Washington, and West Virginia); Department of Commerce (Arizona, Indiana, Minnesota, and Oklahoma); and the Wyoming Business Council.

Ten states have a type of Department of Energy independent of other state entities (California, Colorado, Kentucky, Maryland, Nebraska, New York, Oregon, Rhode Island, South Carolina, and Utah). Only seven state energy offices are under the jurisdiction of types of Departments of Natural Resources (Idaho, Iowa, Louisiana, Missouri, Montana, New Mexico, and Pennsylvania). Two are located in a Department of Administration (North Carolina and Wisconsin) and two are located in a Department of Facilities (Delaware and Georgia). The others are under the jurisdiction of completely different agencies, such as the Office of Policy and Management (Connecticut), the Board of Public Utilities (New Jersey), the Comptroller of Public Accounts (Texas), the Department of Mines, Minerals and Energy (Virginia), and the Kansas Corporation Commission. Appendix 1 provides the Web address for each state energy office.

The clear link between energy policy and economic interests is evident in the fact that almost half the state energy offices are housed in departments that foster economic development or commerce. Six of these states are also energy resource producers (Illinois, Ohio, West Virginia, Indiana, Oklahoma, and Wyoming) indicating an emphasis on marketing for indigenous fuels as a focus of state energy policy.

We looked at the correlation between the location of energy offices and the individual state's progress toward electricity restructuring. Figure 6.1 shows the status of electricity restructuring activity in the states as of February 2003. The only change in the map after June 2001 was

Table 7.1

State Energy Office Location and Electricity Restructuring

State	Energy office location
Arizona	Department of Commerce
Arkansas	Industrial Development Commission
California	California Energy Commission
Connecticut	Office of Policy and Management
Delaware	Division of Facilities Management
Illinois	Department of Commerce and Community Affairs
Maine	Department of Economic and Community Development
Massachusetts	Department of Economic Development
Michigan	Department of Consumer and Industry Services
Montana	Department of Environmental Quality
Nevada	Department of Business and Industry
New Hampshire	Governor's Office of Energy and Community Services
New Jersey	Board of Public Utilities
New Mexico	Energy, Minerals, and Natural Resources Department
New York	State Energy Research and Development Corporation
Ohio	Department of Development
Oklahoma	Department of Commerce
Oregon	Office of Energy
Pennsylvania	Department of Environmental Protection
Rhode Island	State Energy Office
Texas	Comptroller of Public Accounts
Virginia	Department of Mines, Minerals, and Energy
West Virginia	Development Office

for West Virginia and Oregon. Oregon is now actively restructuring electricity, and West Virginia has discontinued restructuring. The location of the energy office does not appear to correlate with restructuring activity in those states that have completed legislation, as shown in Table 7.1. Of the twenty-three states that had begun to restructure, only ten had energy offices in Departments of Commerce or Economic Development.

More important, perhaps, is that twelve of these states have indigenous energy resources (coal: Illinois, Montana, Ohio, Pennsylvania, Virginia, and West Virginia; gas and oil: California, Oklahoma, and Texas; oil shale: Nevada and New Mexico; renewables: California and Oregon).

Of the states where there was active consideration of restructuring, seven out of eighteen are resource-rich (coal: Colorado, Indiana, Kentucky, and Wyoming; gas and oil: Alaska and Louisiana; renewables: Washington). Of the eight states that had made no movement toward deregulation (Alabama, Georgia, Hawaii, Idaho, Kansas, Nebraska, South Dakota, Tennessee), only Kansas, with large deposits of natural gas, has significant supplies of indigenous energy resources, although Tennessee benefits from the presence of the Tennessee Valley Authority.

This study did not attempt to develop correlates with such factors as political parties of the governor and the legislature, or the influence of the business community. A glance at the map reveals that a high percentage of the early states that deregulated had at least a Republican governor (Arizona, California, Connecticut, Illinois, Maine, Massachusetts, Michigan, Nevada, New Mexico, New York, Ohio, Pennsylvania, Texas, and Virginia). Many of these states also have energy resource industries or electricity providers.

Missions of State Energy Offices

When we examined the mission statements of the energy offices, we found uniformity of emphasis on energy efficiency regardless of location, although their purposes vary. The Texas State Energy Conservation Office (SECO) mission statement provides a historical context of the birth of state energy offices, specifically with regard to funding:

> Created in response to the Arab oil embargo of 1973 and the resulting national energy crisis, the Texas energy office has evolved from its original function of responding to state fuel shortage emergencies and administering federal energy conservation grants to its current role as a statewide promoter of energy efficiency and provider of energy management services, which [has] a positive impact on state energy expenditures and local property tax rates. The primary funding source for SECO programs has been oil overcharge settlements of alleged violations of price controls in effect for crude oil and refined petroleum products between 1973 and 1981. While the U.S. Department of Energy is the federal agency responsible for ensuring compliance with the court settlements, the state's responsibility is to return these funds to the citizens of Texas through promoting and supporting energy efficiency and renewable energy programs according to state and federal guidelines.

The mission statement of New Mexico's Energy Conservation and Management Division, under the auspices of the Energy, Minerals, and Natural Resources Department, is succinct: "encouraging efficient energy use in New Mexico by offering programs and information for state agencies, companies, and individuals."

The mission of Ohio's Office of Energy Efficiency is more visionary in that it states a broader justification for the work it does: "It is an essential government function and public purpose of the state to promote the efficient utilization of energy . . . for the creation of jobs and employment opportunities, the encouragement of economic growth, the promotion of the general welfare, the protection of public health and safety, and the protection of environmental quality."

Several states have an especially strong economic emphasis in their missions. For example, Indiana's Energy Policy Division of the Department of Commerce states: "By improving the energy efficiency of Indiana businesses, we can improve their ability to compete in the marketplace; by improving the energy efficiency of Indiana's consumers, we can increase their spending and saving powers." Tennessee's Department of Economics and Community Development Energy Division talks of the ripple effects that energy efficiency has on the economy: " . . . every dollar that is spent on energy efficiency rather than consumption is reflected exponentially in local economic growth."

Typical phrases found in state energy office mission statements include: management of energy; development of science and technology; efficient energy systems; grants; management, conservation, compliance, and enforcement; environmentally sound; and financially viable.

Programs of State Energy Offices

State energy offices vary in their levels of activity and in the programs they offer to the public and businesses. State energy office programs are shown below according to type of program and number of states offering them. Table 7.2 identifies the types of activities for each kind of program and the number of states that report the activity as part of their energy program.

First order programs are those that have traditionally been part of energy programs since the 1970s. The majority of states offer many of these programs. The low number of states offering weatherization and recycling programs is surprising and may mean that these programs are offered by other state agencies. Second order programs are those offered by a few states and tend to be focused on state-specific interests. Third order programs use emerging technologies to improve energy efficiency and focus on global energy issues. Because states may have activities that overlap these categories, it is not possible to identify individual states as subscribing exclusively to one type of program. Appendix

Table 7.2

State Energy Program Activities by Category

Program category	Activities (no. of states providing each)
First order	Residential and commercial energy efficiency codes and standards (19)
	Consumer tips on energy efficiency (29)
	Weatherization assistance (12)
	Primary and secondary school energy education programs (8)
	Technical assistance and energy audits of residential and commercial buildings and schools (23)
	Energy tax credits, low-interest loans, or grants for energy efficiency for residential and commercial buildings and schools (20)
	Transit programs, including carpooling, vanpooling, ride sharing, alternative fuel vehicles (26)
	Alternative energy development (34)
	Recycling, including compost education (9)
Second order	Statistics on state energy usage (8)
	Air resources management (7)
	Water resources management (8)
	Industry-specific energy efficiency programs[a] (8)
	Treatment, storage, disposal of low-level radioactive waste, and brownfields cleanup (7)
Third order	Technical assistance for businesses on telecommuting (2)
	Training energy management personnel to monitor or control energy consumption (5)
	Software packages for municipalities to track energy use and costs (6)
	Teaming with a university to undertake special energy projects (7)
	Sustainable development/smart growth initiatives (3)

[a]Seafood industry (Alaska), cruise industry (Florida), coal industry (Illinois), aquaculture (North Carolina), swine waste bioremediation (North Carolina), mine subsidence insurance (Pennsylvania), farm methane project (Vermont), glass industry (West Virginia).

2 provides the list of states that offer each program activity. Electricity programs are discussed in a separate section.

Colorado, New Mexico and Oregon focus on global environmental issues and are taking the lead in developing carbon dioxide emissions standards, smart growth initiatives, and sustainable development programs. Colorado's Office of Smart Growth offers technical assistance to local governments dealing with the impact of growth. Such assistance includes developing a vision, land use planning, policies and regulations.

In addition, the office maintains a list of mediators upon whom munici-palities can call to settle disputes.

New Mexico's Energy Conservation and Management Office ties its pollution prevention program to sustainable development. The pollu-tion prevention program promotes the efficient use of natural resources and reduction of waste by assisting businesses in identifying and imple-menting strategies.

Oregon's Office of Energy leads the nation in reducing energy facil-ity carbon dioxide emissions. The office has a detailed energy facility siting process and partners with a nonprofit organization that buys car-bon dioxide offsets with funds provided by power plant developers.

Several states provide grants to local colleges or universities for a variety of energy programs. Some examples are: the University of Ala-bama provides technical assistance to industries on reducing energy costs; North Carolina Agricultural and Technical State University undertakes research in energy use and efficiency in buildings and industrial pro-cesses; Emory University provides electric shuttle service in Atlanta; Maryland Energy Institute offers an energy management curriculum through community colleges and provides technical assistance to local governments on purchasing energy; University of South Carolina School of Environmental Engineering builds a sustainable Habitat for Human-ity home; Clemson University offers a landscape design program for energy efficiency; and the University of Texas installs photovoltaic cells above a garage. Such state programs, if adopted nationwide, might make it possible for the United States to achieve the reductions required by the Kyoto Agreement on carbon dioxide emissions, without serious eco-nomic dislocation.

State Electricity Programs

Traditional state electricity program components include using the En-ergy Star rating program for energy-efficient appliances; conducting energy audits of government buildings, schools, homes, and businesses; providing building codes for energy efficiency; and developing renew-able energy sources such as wind, biomass, and solar power. Public utili-ties have promoted demand-side management (DSM) and utilized integrated resource planning since the early 1980s. Both are vehicles to help utilities offset rising demand and reduce the need to construct new generating plants.

These programs were halted with the breakup of the utilities as part of deregulation. Companies in a deregulated market no longer have any incentive to promote conservation or efficiency. In California, DSM had slowed the rate of electricity demand by 15 percent between 1983 and 1996. These programs stopped when deregulation began because the plants were no longer owned by a regulated utility.

Intergovernmental Aspects of State Energy Programs

While states demonstrably are taking responsibility for their own energy futures, the role of federal policy is still significant. The Energy Policy Act of 1992, which made electricity deregulation possible, also established a federal role in funding and supporting state energy management programs. All fifty states have received grants and programmatic support for their energy offices over the past decade. Several states were still using oil overcharge funds, derived from court decisions of the early 1980s, to fund their energy programs. Many states identified the program Rebuild America as one of their activities. This program was developed and funded by the U.S. Department of Energy to create public-private partnerships to redevelop inner city areas. Energy management is one of the elements of the program. Continued funding for state energy offices and programs like Rebuild America is uncertain, given the Bush II administration's energy policy priorities for energy development and the free market. The 2003 budget for the Department of Energy reduced Rebuild America to funding weatherization alone.

Conclusion

While nineteen states have deregulated electricity, the study of state energy office Web sites identifies the broad interests that encompass state energy policy. These interests have not changed significantly over the past thirty years, except for the addition of programs to promote sustainable development and carbon dioxide reduction. States' energy policy goals continue to include the complex of affordability for all customers, sufficient available supply to meet the needs of current residents and businesses, and environmental protection in a variety of forms.

States, by and large, lose control over this complex of policy interests when one segment of energy is turned over to the market. States cannot risk the loss of control over these interests as markets rise and fall either through the business cycle or manipulation of the market. The primary value of regulation for the states lies in the ability to plan and manage all of these policy interests.

Even as California became the first state to turn electricity provision over to the free market, the state's immediate response to the crisis was to step in to defend its fundamental energy policy goals and protect its complex interests. Other states, watching California, pulled back from implementing deregulation. In those that did open their markets, many found that prices did not fall as predicted and competitors did not rush in to serve residential and commercial customers. Even in the economic downturn since 2001, electricity prices have not fallen, despite the fact that supply now exceeds demand.

This chapter has documented that state energy policy interests have remained constant for thirty years. The reaction of other states to the California electricity crisis and the continued funding of energy efficiency programs in the states demonstrate that the states do have energy policy interests that differ from those of the market. The next chapter discusses the market's interests and the fundamental conflicts that exist between the market and the states.

8

The Market and the States

The companies didn't do anything wrong. That's
the way the market works.
  —*Jeffrey Skilling, then-CEO of Enron Corporation, speaking to Lowell Bergman on*
  Frontline, *broadcast by PBS, June 5, 2001*

Public policymakers have been persuaded since the early 1980s to turn
many government functions over to the market on the premise that the
market is the most efficient way to achieve policy goals as well as to
make and sell products and services. This chapter examines the evolution of market-driven public policy and the assumptions of market theory.
The interests of the market are evaluated in relation to the interests of
the State[1] to address the question of what happens to the public interest
in a market driven by profit. In other words, how does the market work
and can the State protect the public interest through the market?

Economics and Public Policy

Until the late 1970s, U.S. policymakers assumed that there were public
interests that could not be met by the market, and, consequently, had to be
met by government, either through direct service provision or through
regulation—government intervention in the marketplace. Economists even
define "public goods" as those services and products that the market either cannot or will not provide because of the lack of profit opportunity.

Regulation was developed initially to overcome so-called market failures that resulted in monopoly or predatory pricing or restraint of trade.[2]
Regulation increased during the 1930s as the Franklin D. Roosevelt administration worked to stabilize the economy after the 1929 collapse of

99

the stock market. Laws established at that time governed banking and securities, aviation, and communications. Regulatory law protected companies as well as the public from unfair business practices.

The next wave of regulatory policy development came in the 1970s. Regulations enacted in this decade focused on protecting individual rights to clean air and water, workplace health and safety, and consumer product safety. These regulations imposed significant costs on business while the benefits accrued to individuals outside of the firm. At the time, regulators generally employed command-and-control enforcement methods that required all companies in an industry to meet the same standards regardless of individual circumstances, and the costs of compliance rose dramatically.

Regulation came under increasing attack in the 1970s from economists who argued that government was imposing unreasonable costs on business and producing little benefit. A better way, they asserted, would be to use market incentives to encourage businesses to achieve regulatory goals. Then the market could work efficiently to achieve policy goals at much lower cost than the cumbersome command-and-control methods of the government bureaucracy.

The economics argument coupled with questioning of government efficiency in general began to reach sympathetic ears in both political parties, and the idea of deregulation as a policy gained momentum. Deregulation of transportation—trucking and the airlines—was initiated in the Carter administration. Ronald Reagan's administration expanded on this base and brought an ideological preference for free markets to the forefront of government.

There was an international movement toward privatization of government services at that time. The Thatcher government in Britain complemented the interests of the Reaganites and free market conservatism seemed to be sweeping the world. Economists were appointed to high-level positions in the U.S. government; economics theory began to supersede democratic theory in schools of public administration. Murray Weidenbaum, an economics professor who became Chair of Reagan's Council of Economic Advisers, argued that all government programs should be subjected to cost-benefit analysis (Weidenbaum 1981). E.S. Savas's book on privatization of government services (1983) became a widely used text in public administration programs and a guide for government at all levels. Services that governments had provided for over seventy years began to be contracted out to private providers.

The underlying rationale for privatization and deregulation was the quest for efficiency. Government, it was argued, is inherently inefficient because it does not have a bottom line and it is a monopoly. Furthermore, any government bureaucracy is weighed down with policies and procedures as well as unnecessary paperwork that only add to the costs of whatever they do. The private sector is far more efficient, according to this line of thinking, and can provide the same or better quality service at lower costs to the taxpayers.

This logic carried over to the electricity restructuring debate in the early 1990s with the added feature of consumer choice. Government provides only one product—one size fits all at one price. Regulated utilities, although privately owned, offer one product at set prices. The marketplace, on the other hand, offers consumers many choices of the same products at various prices so that they can buy the products they want at the prices they are willing to pay from the vendor they prefer. Why should government interfere in such market transactions? Furthermore, it is alleged, government regulation inhibits the innovation that a free market stimulates by encouraging firms to introduce new and improved products that expand the range of choices for consumers. Regulated companies with a captive market have no incentive to be innovative, so it is assumed.

These arguments lent momentum to the movement to deregulate energy and restructure the electricity industry. The vertical companies were portrayed as fat and complacent because of regulation that assured their profitability even when they made bad investment decisions. They were inefficient, it was said, because they had no incentive to shut down costly generators so long as they could raise rates with government approval. Utility stocks represented a solid investment in many portfolios, but they did not promise the kind of gains that unregulated companies might. They also carried little risk because the companies were guaranteed to make a profit by the states.

The utilities also had few friends among the general population. Both consumer groups and environmentalists criticized the companies for their refusal to alter their ways of doing business. Consumers argued that electricity prices were too high and that they were inequitable, giving large industrial users discounts that were not available to residential users and small businesses. Environmentalists criticized the companies for their pollution, their reluctance to invest in renewable energy, their investments in nuclear power without regard to waste disposal, and pricing policies that encouraged consumption instead of conservation.

These critiques intersected with the deregulation movement in the concept of choice. If the electricity market were opened to choice—retail wheeling—then all consumers could buy electricity at the lowest price. Environmentalists could contract with providers of electricity generated from renewable sources, thus encouraging the market to invest in such facilities. Utilities competing in this market would be forced to innovate to be more efficient and would respond favorably to the demand for cleaner, "greener" energy.

Deregulation, then, fulfills a number of public interests, at least in theory. In the reality of California, however, it failed to meet any of these interests. Was this due to a flawed deregulation plan? Have other states learned from this experience and will deregulation elsewhere be successful? Is this just an isolated case or are there fatal flaws in market theory when it intersects with the State's interests? Is there a fundamental role to be played by government in the marketplace of a great democracy?

How the Market Works

The market is neutral to public interests. It simply operates to provide products that customers will buy. If manufacturers pollute the environment and consumers want a cleaner environment, then they will somehow signal their willingness to pay higher prices for products made with less pollution. Business customers, however, will seek opportunities to reduce costs by moving to states that offer a more beneficial business climate, that is, fewer regulations including pollution control. Equity is not a concern of the market because it is assumed that the mix of goods available will offer something for everyone at prices they can afford to pay. It is also assumed that consumer choice is a matter of preference or willingness to pay and not a matter of economic privation. If consumers were forced because of their poor circumstances to buy only certain products, then they would not really have a choice. Thus, it is generally assumed in economics that what people buy reflects their true desires.

California's experience with electricity deregulation can be seen as typical for a volatile market. Market theory bases prices on the supply and demand of a product. In a market where demand is difficult to predict, as in electricity use, suppliers will try to gauge how much of a product will be needed at a given time so that they do not overproduce. Excess electricity cannot be stored; companies that generate too much will have to sell it at reduced prices, if they can even find a buyer.

The same thing can happen to buyers who contract for delivery of an amount of electricity that exceeds what they need on a given day. They will then be forced to offer the excess to the market at a lower price than they must pay for it. This was another lesson that California's energy managers learned in the summer of 2001. Long-term contracts signed during the height of the crisis, for what seemed like reasonable prices at the time, became white elephants when prices dropped later in the year.

California's deregulation plan prohibited the utilities from entering into long-term contracts for electricity and required that they purchase it from the spot market. The fear of policymakers in 1995 was that the companies would enter into long-term contracts to buy electricity at higher prices than could be obtained on the spot market. Lawmakers were certain that prices would go down with a competitive market and obtaining the lowest prices would be possible only in a day-to-day exchange.

When the spot market demonstrated that prices go up as well as down and generators refused to sell to the utilities because of fears of nonpayment, the state was forced to step in to purchase electricity for the utilities. Economists and energy company executives criticized the state for developing a deregulation plan that foolishly depended on the volatile spot market. So, the California Department of Water Resources was authorized in January 2001 to negotiate long-term electricity contracts at reasonable prices. At that point, "reasonable price" had a very different meaning than it did in the halcyon days of 1995 or during the economic downturn later in 2001.

Negotiators estimated electricity needs based on normal peak demand for summer use and contracted for delivery of sufficient megawatts to meet this demand on a daily basis. Even so, they still forecast energy shortfalls for the summer of 2001 and developed programs to encourage customers to conserve. When electricity use failed to rise to the forecasted levels of demand, the California negotiators were caught with too much supply that could not be sold at the price they were paying for it. Electricity that they were contractually obligated to purchase for $130 per megawatt had to be auctioned off to essentially the lowest bidder—as low as $25 per megawatt—just to offset some of the state's costs.

This is not the result of poor negotiations. It is simply the way the market works. If you try to reduce your risk through long-term agreements, then you have to be prepared to be wrong some of the time. Electricity cannot be stored; it must be distributed as it is produced. So electricity produced for a contract is delivered whether the demand is there or not. That increases the supply on the grid and lowers the price for all other customers. This is, in fact, why the deregulators wanted to prohibit long-term contracts in the first place.

If the state were a corporation, the loss would be a mere bookkeeping entry. Corporations, after all, can afford to make mistakes insofar as they can pass on the costs to their customers or write off a loss on their tax returns. The state, on the other hand, has no way to write off a loss. All of its mistakes are revealed on the front page of the daily newspaper and become the lead story on the six o'clock newscast. Moreover, spending public money on unused electricity draws funds away from other state programs and operations. Spending for education, health care, social services, transportation, and other state programs had to be reduced in California in order to pay for electricity contracts.

States and Market Interests

The studies of state energy policy have shown clearly that the states' energy policy interests are a reliable supply of energy at an affordable price for all users in the state, produced in a manner that is environmentally acceptable. So far, the market has not shown that it can meet these interests or that it even wants to meet them. Both the leaders of the energy industry and the Bush II energy task force[3] demonstrated that to them a sound energy policy would require dotting the countryside with power plants and extracting fuel resources from every piece of ground that might contain a little oil or gas to meet the demand of an energy-hungry market. If we take these leaders to be representative of the market, then we can assert confidently that, at best, the market has different interests than the states, and, at worst, the market's interests are often in conflict with the states' interests.

As we have seen in chapters 3 and 7, the states' basic interests in energy policy have not changed over the past twenty-five years. The states, more than the federal government, are responsible for the well-being of their citizens, their environmental quality, and their economies. While the federal government can look at the macroeconomy from an academic perspective, state governments see it up close.

States also have a responsibility to protect their residents from inequitable treatment or lack of access to necessities. Their concern in energy policy is to make sure that all residents can afford to pay what is necessary to heat, cool, and light their homes. As we saw in the 1992 study, states were far ahead of the national government in beginning to develop policies to deal with global warming. The states, then, have concerns that override those of the national government and the free market.

The Market and Social Values

American industry is extremely successful at flooding the marketplace with all kinds of goods that may or may not have any social value, but they all carry some kind of social cost. Environmental pollution is a major social cost of electricity generation. Government regulation requires companies to make huge investments in environmental control technology, although the Clean Air Act now authorizes the use of economic incentives such as emissions trading to help companies choose the most efficient method of cleanup and control.

Economists argue that if the public really wants a cleaner environment they will show their willingness to pay higher prices for products that are produced in an environmentally safe manner or that operate more efficiently. Yet most consumers do not have that information when making a purchase and lower prices do influence their shopping choices. In energy use, higher prices have been shown to be a strong incentive for conservation, but deregulation promises to lower prices, thus counteracting efficiency and conservation.

During the late 1970s and early 1980s, high energy prices and government subsidies led Americans to lower energy demand significantly through conservation and the use of renewable energy. The demand for small efficient cars, most of which were built by foreign companies, convinced American companies to offer their own lines. Gasoline demand fell so low that the prices of Organization of Petroleum Exporting Countries cartel collapsed. Higher pricing also spurred demand for energy-efficient building materials and appliances to ameliorate the effects of high heating and cooling bills.

Regulation of electricity was originally conceived as necessary to overcome another kind of market failure, the high costs of competition in a market where companies could not be certain of making a fair rate of return. State regulation made it possible for utilities to earn fair rates of return from a guaranteed customer base. Deregulation was made possible when the companies could expand that base beyond state borders and when small generators became economically viable.

One of the fundamental functions of the regulation of electricity is to manage supply so that it can meet the demand within the state throughout the year. Excess capacity is built to provide sufficient electricity to meet peak demand needs for summer air conditioning. These "peakers" sit idle or operate at reduced capacity until their production is needed. Plant maintenance is managed so that sufficient capacity will be available while some generators are off-line. Utilities in California invested in conservation and efficiency programs where it could be shown that they "produced" supply more cheaply than building new power plants. They also managed capacity so that generating capacity could be added as demand increased.

Coordinated planning was lost as soon as deregulation became a real possibility. With a free market there is no central management of supply and demand. Energy companies want to sell as much product as they can at the highest price they can get. There is no mechanism for ensuring that the capacity will be available when and where it is needed. Companies do not build "peakers" because idle capacity would increase costs and reduce efficiency. Nor is there any incentive for any company to encourage a customer to conserve, that is, use less product. Consequently, the message to consumers is to buy and use products that require electricity with no regard to the latter's future availability.

The Profit Imperative

What happened in California is simply a consequence of the "profit imperative." Profit is all that counts to American corporations and their shareholders. There is really very little to prevent companies from selling anything that will produce a profit, regardless of its social costs. I often tell my students about my experience as a young market researcher in a Fortune 500 chemical company in the early 1960s. At that time, the fastest growing market in the chemical industry was disposable packaging. Chemical companies were madly competing to develop all kinds of packaging: shrink-wrap, blister packs, coated papers, soft drink bottles, and so forth. I asked my supervisor one day how "we" would dispose of all this stuff. His response was "That's not the industry's problem. It's government's problem." Clearly the solid waste produced by these companies has indeed become a major problem for governments. We often think that America has always been a "disposable society," but, as this story illustrates, we have been encouraged to become so by the market.

The quest for profits requires a continual effort to convince consumers to spend. Appliances are built with a limited life expectancy (planned obsolescence) so that they have to be replaced often—more appliance sales. Product models are frequently changed (new and improved) to entice consumers to buy again. Advertising shows us that we "need" things we never thought about before. And if we do not have the cash, there is always a credit card company willing to help us out.[4]

The U.S. economy is consumer driven; it depends on consumers to continuously spend so that companies can keep making higher and higher profits and the economy can grow. The market cannot care about social equity or environmental costs so long as it must focus on the profit imperative. Any requirements to internalize these costs will reduce profits. At the height of the energy crisis in California, energy companies were posting huge profits and were the darlings of Wall Street investors. Pacific Gas and Electric (PG&E) Corporation posted record third-quarter profits in October 2001 while still working to bail out its retail company from bankruptcy.

The market sends signals to consumers to overconsume. New products are introduced all the time. Through mass media, Americans at all economic levels are shown the things that are deemed necessary for a prosperous lifestyle. Fifty years ago, the distinctions between rich and poor were not so clear. People who came through the Great Depression and World War II tell us that they did not really know that they were poor. Today television and newer technologies project images that readily demonstrate the products needed to show that one is not poor. Advertising tells us what we need to live the good life. Poor children today know that they are poor and still demand the same expensive shoes and electronic toys that rich children have.

Since 1945, the economy in this country has grown impressively. The standard of living, measured as gross domestic product per capita, is the highest in the world and in the history of the world. This measure, however, is really a dollar measure of how much stuff is produced and owned in this country and not a qualitative measure of living. It is not balanced against the costs of commuting long distances to get to work in order to pay for the big house in the suburbs, the electric and electronic gadgets it holds, and the SUV used to get there and back. These costs, too, are folded into the GDP and standard of living calculation. These are actually hidden costs of the consumer market.

During the electricity crisis, Californians were portrayed as energy hogs, crying about having to pay too much for electricity for frivolous uses like hot tubs and computer gadgets. Yet, these products are used all over the country, even in climates where it takes much more electricity to heat a hot tub. It is fair to ask, I think, whether Americans are energy pigs or market victims. If the market offers products that use electricity without any concern for the increasing power demand that they collectively represent, are consumers at fault if they then create that demand? Should consumers not expect that the electricity to operate these products would continue to be provided at low prices? Is that implicit in the explosion of electricity-using products? Or is this just another one of "government's problems?"

Market theory tells us that energy-producing companies will rush in to produce the electricity needed for growing demand. Yet that did not happen in California. The companies instead reaped huge profits from their existing supplies and then castigated the state government for not encouraging the building of new power plants in the state. But this leads to another question about how the market is supposed to work. If consumers in a deregulated market can buy electricity from any provider in the country and most of the continent, then why does the state have to have its own sources of electricity? Is the market not supposed to meet this demand? If the state has to guarantee that power will be available within its borders, then why should the state not also regulate the industry to ensure that generating capacity will be available when needed? Furthermore, in an unregulated market, in-state power plants are under no obligation to sell their product locally if they can get a better price outside the state. Residents of Oregon and Washington learned this basic lesson during the height of the California crisis, when their prices shot up as supply in the state dropped while the companies rushed to serve the California market.

This case also demonstrates that the market does not care *how* profits are made. Many companies today do not make products or offer direct services to consumers, they just make money. The energy wholesale generators are a prime example of this phenomenon. Most do not produce electricity themselves but are brokers—middlemen—who buy electricity from producers and then sell it to retail customers at the highest price they can command. They are under no obligation to offer all the electricity they have available to the market at any given time but can withhold supply until they can get a better price. Because their only product is money, they will seek the greatest financial gain they can.

This is apparently part of what happened in California. Energy companies seized the opportunity to gain huge profits by limiting the supply available to the market. Demand did not rise significantly in the winter of 2001, but supply fell off sharply and prices for megawatts rose dramatically. This was done partly by taking generating capacity off-line for maintenance. It was also done by deliberately withholding capacity when it was needed most. The independently owned utilities and the customers were left with no alternative but to pay whatever the market demanded for a necessary product. This resulted in a massive shift of wealth from the state and consumers to a few large energy companies, mostly in Texas.

In this kind of market, consumer choice cannot be said to be sovereign. There was no low price alternative available. Consumers could not choose *not* to buy the product. Consequently, it cannot be argued that this represents a truly free market. Free markets work only where there is complete freedom on the part of sellers *and* buyers to participate in the market. Where buyers must accept whatever is offered, there is no choice. Where sellers can set prices that are not affected by competition, there is no free transaction in the market. This is precisely the problem that Samuel Insull foresaw in supporting regulation of the electricity industry in the beginning. This is also why many economists and state policymakers are now questioning whether electricity deregulation is good public policy.

The State Interest vs. the Market Interest

Markets are relatively simple, according to conventional theory, but states are complex. State governments operate in a political environment that must meet competing public needs in order to maintain economic and political stability. Political leaders must be sensitive to the interests of various constituencies and must have a concern for equity. It is said that politics is about who gets what, where, and how. Politicians who make the wrong decisions about these factors can jeopardize their own careers.

The policy to restructure electricity in California was developed in response to the demands of one political interest—large energy users that threatened to leave the state unless electricity prices were reduced—and a political ideology that fit well with the then-governor's ambitions for national office. The final policy was designed to gain the support of many other interests: the utilities, consumer groups, small businesses, environmental groups, and so forth. All were dazzled by the market promise of cheaper electricity rates all around and choice of electricity provider. When the market failed to deliver on this promise, the impacts on state political leaders, especially the governor, were severe.[5] Only then did policymakers recognize the importance of the other interests at stake in energy policy.

A projected $10 billion state budget surplus was used to purchase electricity. This, along with a faltering state economy, resulted in budget cuts for state programs such as education, transportation, and so forth. The state economy, already suffering from the collapse of the dot-coms, was hit again as the cost of doing business in the state escalated because of energy costs. Energy prices are not isolated to individuals but spread throughout the fabric of the economy. Higher business costs get passed on to consumers and other businesses so that the impact of price hikes is magnified. Higher government and nonprofit operating costs take resources away from programs and strain government budgets. Higher energy prices reduce consumers' spending on other products, further contributing to economic decline.

The interests of the state are thus compromised by the interests of the market. Where the state has an interest in equitable prices for all consumers, rich and poor alike, the market is interested only in maximizing profits, whether by selling more at lower prices where demand is increasing or selling less at higher prices where demand is steady or declining. Where the state has an interest in protecting the environment, for reasons of public health and aesthetic value, the market is interested only in reducing production costs by externalizing wastes (pollution) as much as possible. Where the state has an interest in strengthening the economy within its borders, the market does not care where customers operate so long as they keep buying the product. These are the fundamental conflicts between the market and the state.

The risks inherent in market dynamics are precisely the reason that governments should examine carefully the pros and cons of privatization and deregulation. It is not purely a political issue, although the electricity crisis surely threatened Governor Gray Davis's political fortunes, but it is an issue of market failure. A market failure occurs when the market either cannot or will not provide a product that the public needs. Government then steps in to offer services that are perceived to be in the public interest.

The California electricity crisis was not a market failure, but, rather, a huge market success. The market operates on one principle: the profit imperative. As long as companies can make a profit, the market is working. And the higher the profits, the better it works. Damage to the public interest is of no concern to the market, for it will charge whatever a consumer is desperate enough to pay.

Throughout the winter of 2001, the front pages and editorial sections of California newspapers printed hand-wringing articles every day about the power crisis. Back in the business sections of these same papers were reports gleefully heralding the huge increases in profits garnered by Enron, Duke Energy, and the other energy brokers, including California-based companies, PG&E Corporation and Calpine. The companies have no interest in selling the product at an affordable rate so long as there is a customer who will pay more, as residents of Washington State and British Columbia discovered.

If California were to go dark because its utilities are bankrupt, then that would just be the fallout of a free market freely operating. The public interest is of no value to the market, although one might question whether it is good business practice to bankrupt a state that ranks as the fifth largest economy in the world.

Conclusion

The fallout from the winter of 2001 had not been settled almost two years later. At the end of June 2003, the state was still trying to recover billions of dollars in overcharges from energy companies through the Federal Energy Regulatory Commission (Federal Energy Regulatory Commission 2003). Other states advertise to entice California companies to relocate where electricity is cheaper and supply more reliable. Retail customers in California now face electricity prices that are 40 percent or more higher than they were before deregulation, and there is no belief that they will come down any time soon.

In September 2001, the California Public Utility Commission eliminated retail customer choice in order to ensure that the utilities would have enough ratepayers at the new higher rates to pay off their debts. Earlier in the summer, however, when wholesale prices fell, the large users signed contracts with energy providers to escape the higher rates of investor-owned utilities. This effectively passes on the majority of the costs of the deregulation debacle to residential and small business ratepayers. Nettie Hoge, executive director of the Utility Reform Network of San Francisco said, "Big business wanted deregulation, but when it resulted in skyrocketing prices, they were the first to bail. Now, they want to give it another shot—at our expense." (Mitchell 2001: Business-5).

In the end, California's experience struck a major blow against the idea of electricity deregulation itself. States that were in the process of restructuring began to put safeguards in place and other states began to rethink the whole idea of deregulation. It is unlikely that the old vertical industry will be resurrected—there were problems with the regulated industry as well. What is certain, in my view, is that government at all levels will have to examine more carefully the public interest (and political interests) before turning essential public services over to a volatile, greedy marketplace. In the next chapter, we consider whether it is possible to achieve a balance between the interests of the market and the states.

9

Balancing the Interests of the States and the Market

Deregulation as public policy is a powerful idea that is not going away any time soon. Given the conflict between the market's interests and the public's interests, however, deregulation without government oversight seems imprudent. This chapter examines whether it is possible to develop a balanced policy that can enable the market to work effectively while achieving nonmarket public policy interests. I try to propose such a balance that matches the strengths of the market with the public policy interests of the state. I raise more questions than I can provide answers to. Perhaps that is just as well, as good public policy derives from the interactions of many interests in the political arena not just the ideas of one analyst or one theory.

What Is Good About Regulation?

Regulation began in the United States in the 1880s as a reaction to predatory market practices of the railroads. The Interstate Commerce Commission, the first regulatory agency, was established primarily to overcome market abuses and establish a level playing field for both companies and customers. The purpose of regulation since then, seen in such agencies as the Food and Drug Administration, the Securities and Exchange Commission, and the Federal Communications Commission, has been to overcome excesses in the market and to compensate for market failure. As we have seen, the pioneers of the electricity industry believed that it should be regulated as a natural monopoly. During the New Deal era, the industry was vertically integrated so that single companies provided all electrical services, from generation to transmission to retail distribution. With states providing oversight of companies within their borders, the industry thrived. California's companies were among the best in the country for both consumers and shareholders. They collaborated well with state regulators to meet the demands of a diverse and growing state economy.

Was Deregulation Necessary?

Daniel Fessler, chair of the California Public Utility Commission, proposed deregulation policy in California in response to the demands of the big electricity users. It was not immediately embraced by most sectors in the state, and, in fact, was initially opposed by the utilities themselves. To most citizens, even today, it is not clear that the electricity industry in California was in need of fixing. The rush to develop deregulation policy to meet a theoretical ideal—free market efficiency—was clearly a serious mistake, at least as the policy was written. Today's retail customers are much worse off than they would have been had regulation continued as it was in 1996. So, from the viewpoint of the majority of customers—residential, commercial, and small business—deregulation probably was not necessary. Up to now, in any case, they have gained no benefit and, in fact, have suffered losses. Electricity costs have risen by 40 percent, small customers have no choice of provider, and the retail electricity companies themselves have declined in market value. Among the biggest losers of deregulation were the thousands of PG&E shareholders and retirees who lost their nest eggs when the company filed for bankruptcy.

On the other hand, vertical integration of the industry does seem like an anachronism when electronic communication systems have made it possible to buy and sell electrons at great distances. The production of electricity can be separated from transmission and retail distribution. Why, then, should it not be freely traded the way other commodities are? Why should the state dictate how the business operates any more than it governs how pork bellies are traded. If Company X in Kansas has excess generating capacity to sell to Company Z in Arizona, why should this transaction not be made like any other market transaction without government intervention?

If selling electricity itself can be done by the market, what of the remainder of the vertical industry, transmission and retail distribution? Transmission does seem to fit the model of a natural monopoly. It is difficult to envision in this segment of the industry competition that would not involve multiple wires and transmission towers crisscrossing the countryside. This would be enormously expensive and inefficient as well as aesthetically ugly and probably dangerous. In addition, maintaining and managing the transmission grid requires coordination that would not be possible in a competitive market.

Continuing monopoly ownership of transmission systems seems to be the best option for the market as well as the public. What is not clear, however, is whether that ownership should be private or public. There is an argument to be made for state ownership of the transmission grid, perhaps with management of the system contracted out to private companies. Government ownership would ensure that all private companies retain access to the grid and avoid the possibility of monopoly power being exerted by the utilities to exclude certain providers. The government would also be able to identify critical development needs for electricity transmission and to strategically plan the growth and expansion of the system. Because the transmission system must be open to all competitors, there seems to be no persuasive argument for it being owned by the independently owned utilities (IOUs). Government ownership may better facilitate the workings of the market, especially if the system were established as a public authority with its own budgeting and bonding capability.

That leaves retail distribution as the remaining segment of the regulated industry. Because this segment includes maintenance of the wires that carry electricity to individual locations, this would seem to be the most likely candidate for continued ownership by the IOUs. They have the equipment and organizational infrastructure to continue to operate these systems efficiently. They would continue to be regulated monopolies to prevent price gouging. On the other hand, there is no reason that this function could not also become a public enterprise, following the example of successful public electricity providers like Los Angeles Water & Power and the Sacramento Municipal Utility District (SMUD). During the crisis, customers of these local government-owned corporations saw no price increases and no blackouts. Municipally owned companies have traditionally provided power for their people, responding to public demand to protect regional interests, as well. In the 1990s, SMUD decommissioned a nuclear generator following a citizen referendum in which voters approved a rate hike in order to cover the generator's stranded costs.

Local governments all over the state of California began to consider public power options following the crisis. Some studied the possibility of developing a municipal utility district that would generate its own power. Others considered becoming exempt wholesale generators to contract with providers for wholesale electricity that they would then sell at retail to their own citizens. The citizens of San Francisco narrowly defeated an initiative in 2001 that would have allowed the city to take over the PG&E system through eminent domain. East Bay Municipal Utility District in Oakland, which provides water to a large population, held public meetings to discuss the possibility of becoming an electricity utility as well. The greatest irony to come out of electricity deregulation could be local governments entering the market that they had previously stayed out of because the regulated industry provided reliable service at an affordable price.

What Is Good About Deregulation?

Regulation seems like an anachronism in an advanced global economy. As competition expands with companies outside the borders of the state and the nation, regulation seems to be increasingly restrictive. Deregulation promises the opportunity for innovation, new products, and technological change. Regulation, on the other hand, supports the status quo and can reward companies for what would be considered bad investment decisions in a free market. So the supporters of deregulation point out that regulated electricity utilities invested in expensive nuclear generation facilities only because they were guaranteed a return on their investment that might not have been possible in a competitive situation. These investments drove up the price of electricity while the companies amortized their costs. In a free market, companies that make poor investments would falter in the face of competitors who kept their operating costs low so they could offer consumers lower prices, too.

That is the theory, at least. The evidence to support it is not always convincing. Regulated companies in the past had solid reputations as efficient and innovative operations. Bell Laboratories, for example, was among the most creative and innovative research centers in the world when it was part of the regulated AT&T. Today as Lucent Technologies, it has foundered and is dangerously close to going out of business altogether. The regulated public utilities were solid, reliable investments in the portfolios of many retirees, pension plans, and other mutual funds.

Even though they were regulated, they returned dependable profits. They were able to manage their businesses in such a way that they provided a reliable product at an acceptable price and still provided dividends for their shareholders. Part of the fallout from the California electricity crisis was the loss of the pension and retirement income of thousands of PG&E employees and ordinary investors, many of them senior citizens who saw their retirement income decline. These were long-term investors in the original company that was spun off under deregulation as the retail distribution arm. It was this segment of the company that filed for bankruptcy. The parent companies that are now exempt wholesale generators made huge profits while their operating subsidiaries were going bankrupt. The new companies represent a riskier investment, however, because profits are linked to the volatile electricity-trading market that did not exist before deregulation.

The market can offer consumers choices that the regulated monopolies did not, and it can send signals about consumer interests and willingness to pay for products. Consumers can create markets for "green" electricity and non-nuclear electricity if given the opportunity to contract directly with companies that supply electricity made from renewable resources. In California, the "green" provider Green Mountain Energy Company attracted significant numbers of customers who were willing to pay slightly higher prices for environmentally benign electricity. No other provider had the success in the California market that Green Mountain did. In reality, California residents did not have many choices, and most customers chose to stay with their IOU. This may indicate that they were generally satisfied with the services offered by the IOUs—demonstrating again that residential customers were not convinced that the system was broken before deregulation.

Since California policymakers decided against retail wheeling, in order to gain the political support of the utilities, provider choice may not have been seen as a true choice by most consumers. Customers still received their bills from the old company so choice may have seemed overly complex. Those who did choose an alternate provider received two bills each month, one from the provider for the electricity and one from the utility for distribution costs. Table 9.1 shows the actual January 2001 electricity bills for our household from Green Mountain Energy and PG&E.

They demonstrate among other things why PG&E was forced into bankruptcy. The Green Mountain bill is succinct—kilowatt hours used

Table 9.1

Household Electricity Bills for January 2001

a. *Green Mountain Energy*

KWh used	519	
Price per KWh	$0.2718960	
Charge	$141.10	
Service charge	6.95	
Total bill	$148.15	

b. *Pacific Gas and Electric*

Transmission		$2.99
Distribution		20.00
Public purpose programs		1.85
Nuclear decommissioning		0.26
Competition transition charge (CTC)		115.10–
Trust transfer amount (TTA)		5.30

Summary

Total charges		$62.58
Legislated 10 percent reduction		6.26–
Direct access energy credit	$0.27187/Kwh	141.10–
Net charges		$84.78–

Price per KWh		
Baseline usage	379.5 @ $0.11589	
Over baseline usage	139.5 @ 0.13321	

(519) and the rate charged (27 cents) plus a monthly service charge. Total charge: $148.15. The PG&E bill, however, is complex. It, too, has a charge for electricity ($62.58), representing the controlled rate that PG&E was allowed to charge, minus the mandated 10 percent reduction, plus the distribution charge and the Competition Transition Charge (CTC) that was designed to pay off PG&E's stranded assets. The CTC was envisioned as an added charge that PG&E could charge until all of its stranded costs were amortized. In this case, however, the CTC is a negative charge that reflects the difference in the market price and the regulated price. Because the maximum allowable price was less than the market price, PG&E *owed* us $84.78 that month. Even now, I do not understand these bills.

This kind of complex accounting might well lead the average consumer to question the benefits of provider choice. Indeed, evidence from New York and California indicates that consumers may not really want as much choice as economists believe they should. Deregulation requires people to make decisions about purchases that were previously simple transactions that were reasonably priced and did not have to be negotiated. Choice brings anxiety and uncertainty along with freedom. In a truly competitive market, one can never be certain that one has obtained the lowest price, whether one is buying a car or choosing a long distance provider. Some social critics now are questioning whether endless choice is even good psychologically and suggest that people may not want to be bothered making choices for every commodity (Johnson 2000).

Ultimately, consumers may begin to question whether deregulation actually delivers on its promises. Are prices really lower in a free market? Are choices really better? Airline deregulation initially brought genuine competition as new companies entered the market and offered low prices on travel that the large airlines could not. The large companies eventually bought up most of these upstarts and the number of major airlines is smaller today than before the industry was deregulated. The hub-city system that airlines use today gives them virtual monopolies at those locations, and the residents of those areas typically pay higher fares than do travelers making a connection there.

Cable television provides another example. The cable industry began in the 1970s as a regulated monopoly. Cities accepted bids from cable service providers that then built the system infrastructure in return for a monopoly to provide service within the community. Deregulation of the cable television industry in the early 1990s was supposed to open the market to multiple providers, provide choice, and bring prices down. What has happened in many regions is that one provider has captured the market although, in theory, other companies can enter the market. The only real competition is from wireless companies that use satellite technology instead of cable. Prices are much higher.

In a competitive market, it is rational behavior for companies to work to reduce the number of competitors, as Mancur Olson demonstrated in his classic *The Logic of Collective Action* (Olson 1965). Too many competitors in a market make it difficult for any one company to maximize its profits. Companies have to gamble on the amount of market share that they can gain, and, consequently, either overproduce or underproduce. If they underproduce, they lose market share they might have had. If they overproduce, supply will exceed demand, which lowers prices and reduces everyone's profits. This is easily seen in agricultural markets where a good year that produces bumper crops leads to lower prices per bushel and thus lower profits for all producers.

Olson argues that markets tend to become oligopolies in which a few large producers dominate and can better control their own market share. Again, the airline industry is a good example of this phenomenon. After deregulation, the presence of many small airlines, offering no frills air travel at very low prices, cut into the market share of large carriers. The large carriers then cut their own prices, while continuing to offer superior service, until they had recovered sufficient market share. Because they had better services, consumers naturally chose to fly the bigger airline for the same price. Eventually the smaller companies folded or were bought out by the big airlines and the number of carriers shrank. In an industry with high costs of operation, it makes sense to reduce competition wherever possible so that profits for the surviving companies will be maximized. There are far fewer airlines today than in 1980 and fewer large airlines as well.

How free is a market where there are only a few providers? The California electricity market, in reality, was not truly competitive. The number of providers was limited at both the wholesale and retail levels, offering an open invitation to the kind of price manipulation that developed. What actually happened in California may have been the trading of a regulated monopoly for a real one or, at best, an oligopoly.

This should not have come as a surprise. Electricity is not a commodity that can be loaded onto a truck and driven somewhere. The practical reality is that electricity transmission must be done in a limited region because of transmission losses over longer distances. For states that are located on the edge of the continent, as California is, access to electrons is limited to those generated in the immediate region. California imports electricity from its neighboring states, Mexico and Canada. States in the middle of the country, on the other hand, have many more options.

Market Failures and Political Failures

There were failures on both sides. Although the market did indeed work for the benefit of the wholesale electricity companies, it clearly failed to meet the needs of retail customers. Policymakers designed the mechanisms that enabled the companies to gain huge profits, but failed to achieve the promises of deregulation. Whether this was a market failure, as economists brand markets that do not operate efficiently, is another question. Several energy companies made huge amounts of profit which is the measure of success in the market. Even if those companies are eventually forced to return some of their profits, they are still likely to have benefited handsomely at the expense of captive customers in California.

It was clearly a policy failure in that deregulation failed to serve the general public interest. Policymakers believed that deregulation would reduce electricity prices through choice so that all consumers in the state would benefit. While some of the elements of the policy were certainly flawed—the Power Exchange for a notable example—choice did not develop in the California market nor have many states attracted multiple providers, as we have seen. Ultimately in California, deregulation itself was a victim as the state moved to protect the energy policy interests that deregulation did not.

The state is now more involved in the electricity market than it ever was under regulation. It is purchasing electricity, promoting and subsidizing conservation, and approving new generating capacity, some of which will be peakers—plants that will provide power during peak usage times or during maintenance closures in the state. As the state expands its role and ensures that in-state generation increases, it is questionable whether the market outside the state will ever play a major role again. It is doubtful that any future governor, at least in the near term, could get the political support needed to return to a market that so badly failed to meet the public's interests.

At the same time, deregulation has unalterably changed the electricity industry in California and most of the country. The regulated utilities no longer exist as they were in many states, and they cannot easily be put back together. The parent companies are making higher profits than were possible under regulation. Many of their generating plants were sold to other companies so that it would be difficult, if not impossible, to restructure the industry again. The companies now have to operate within a deregulated market with considerable state control over their activities.

The remaining issue then is how it might be possible to design public policy that would balance both public and private interests. Can the state protect its fundamental energy policy interests while still enabling companies to make a *reasonable* profit? If the state gets too involved in the market, will the companies abandon the state for greener pastures, states that allow them to make a higher profit? If the state withdraws from market control, will the companies find new ways to generate extraordinary profits? What can the state do to ensure that the companies behave themselves?

The New Role of the State

The most important roles for the state are, first, as planner and coordinator, working with the industry to develop generation facilities in environmentally friendly ways, and, second, as promoter of energy efficiency and conservation to reduce electricity demand within the state. The market cannot be counted on to do either because each company is interested only in maximizing its own profits and not in increasing production until demand has appeared, because to do so would temporarily create excess capacity that would lower prices. Companies generally do not urge customers to use less of their product so we cannot expect them to promote conservation.

Under regulation, the public utilities used to anticipate demand and were able to build facilities in anticipation of demand because they were guaranteed a return on investment even for idle capacity. Companies were also given incentives to promote energy efficiency or demand-side management in the form of a steady profit stream. No company in a free market can afford to operate this way, so it falls to the state to identify growing demand and develop plans for meeting it through either generation or efficiency. The states also have to identify needs for new capacity so that electricity remains available and affordable for all consumers in the state. The California example and others demonstrate that states cannot depend on the market to maintain an affordable supply of electricity.

The state must also continue to develop policies that encourage citizens to adopt energy efficiency as a lifestyle. This is difficult for at least two reasons: market enticements that increase demand and cultural biases that favor consumption. The market depends upon continually increasing demand and profits. There are no regulatory limits on the development of new energy-using products and no mechanism for evaluating the cumulative energy demand that new products represent. As Figure 9.1 shows, U.S. economic growth for the past thirty years has been accompanied by growth in electricity use. The explosion of electronics gadgets beginning in the 1980s is largely responsible for the exponential growth of electricity demand during the 1990s. During the same period, housing developers began building bigger and bigger houses that include more electricity-driven appliances, further stimulating demand. The pressure on consumers is always to use more with no consideration for the true costs of their consumption. Consumers then assume that the commodity, electricity, will always be available in sufficient quantity and at a price they can afford to pay. I leave it to you to decide whether this represents consumer demand or market manipulation.

Figure 9.1 **U.S. Economic Growth as Compared with Electricity Usage**

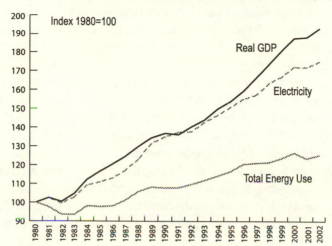

Source: Edison Electronic Institute: www.eei.org. Reprinted with the permission of the Edison Electric Institute.

Consumption in the United States also has a cultural base. As a highly advanced materialistic society, we are measured in some way individually by the amount of stuff we accumulate, and the bigger and more expensive the stuff the better. The growth in sales of SUVs is indicative of this phenomenon. In the San Francisco region and the areas around large cities nationwide, people move to distant suburbs to live in large new houses equipped with the latest electronic gadgetry because they are priced lower than similar housing close to the city. They then spend up to two hours each way driving their SUVs to work in the city or in Silicon Valley or another employment center.

By traditional GDP measures, they have a high standard of living— all of those high-priced things add up to a substantial dollar value. By human measures, I am not so sure. The time spent commuting takes an emotional toll in terms of stress and lost time with the children who are the putative beneficiaries of this wealth. These parents have to work even harder to support the stuff just to keep up the grand lifestyle. During the height of the electricity crisis, some of these homeowners had bills as high as $600 per month for the use of multiple electricity ports for computers, entertainment suites for big screen televisions, home theaters, and stereo equipment.

Obviously, demand exists or the market would not offer this expensive stuff. The underlying philosophy in America is that if I can afford it, I can have it, regardless of the social or environmental costs or whether my excessive use drives up the price for all others in the market. To paraphrase Leona Helmsley's comment about taxes, "Only the little people conserve energy."

When it comes to conservation, however, the market does send the right signal through pricing. When prices are high, conservation makes sense for almost everyone. Unquestionably, the conservation efforts that Californians undertook in the spring and summer of 2001 played a substantial role in bringing down demand and market prices. Californians know how to reduce demand. During the fifteen years preceding deregulation, demand-side management (DSM) programs of the major utilities reduced the growth of demand to such an extent that the actual demand in 1995 was about 15 percent less than it would have been without DSM.

Unfortunately, pricing to encourage conservation is problematic for at least three reasons. First, pricing perpetuates the basic inequities of all free market systems. It is, in essence, forced conservation for the poor who may also be victims of circumstances as energy consumers because they cannot afford to pay for energy and they lack the capital resources to invest in conservation projects that would lower their bills. They must do without rather than investing in ways to do better with less. Ironically, it is the rich who can afford to pay higher energy prices who also have the capital to make energy-saving changes in their habits. The price has to rise to significant levels to make it worth their while to install energy saving devices, and that makes it even harder for the poor.

Second, conservation by pricing is a short-term mechanism that does not lead to permanent reductions in consumption because it does not lead to any basic changes in attitude about energy use. During the 1970s and 1980s, when oil prices hit all time highs, Americans bought smaller, more efficient cars. The automobile manufacturers were required, by government policy, to steadily increase the fuel economy of their vehicles, excluding trucks. After 1982, the price of gasoline did not rise with inflation, however, so by the 1990s, the real price of a gallon was about the same as the price in 1973 when adjusted for inflation. Consumers then began to buy larger vehicles that use more gasoline and automobile manufacturers began to develop SUVs for the average consumer market. Categorized as light trucks, these big and heavy vehicles use significantly more fuel than the small cars that they replace. Drivers love them because they are roomy and safer in a crash. So long as the price of gasoline stays relatively low, there is no reason for consumers to worry about the amount of oil that they demand. As the number of SUVs grows—they are now 50 percent of new vehicle sales per year—so will the pressure on government to keep oil prices down.

In contrast to consumers in other countries that heavily tax gasoline, U.S. consumers enjoy low prices. With the current visceral opposition to taxation in this country, it is unlikely that gasoline taxes will increase substantially anytime soon. In addition, the owners of SUVs will constitute a significant political force against gasoline price increases that might provide the incentive for conservation that would also reduce the demand for SUVs.

The third problem with conservation by pricing is that energy price hikes, even if temporary, are inflationary. Because our production and transportation systems are energy intensive, any increase in fuel or electricity prices leads to a chain reaction of increases in the price of virtually every product and service from breakfast cereal to plastic gewgaws. Operating costs increase for businesses that then pass these costs along to consumers. Government operating costs also increase leading to budget cuts or tax increases as government budgets stretch to reallocate resources to energy. Ultimately, as we see in the California case, price hikes result in a massive shift of wealth from average citizens to a handful of large energy corporations. Using pricing to promote energy conservation, while effective, is costly in other ways and unlikely to be successful in the longer term.

The state of California should also continue to promote the development of alternative energy systems that use the state's most abundant energy resource—sunshine. During the electricity crisis, the state implemented a program to subsidize solar electricity systems for homeowners and commercial businesses, the latter with lobbying by actor Clint Eastwood, who owns a restaurant-hotel complex in Carmel. New policy should be developed to establish self-generating standards for any new industrial building. As an example, a server farm, covering about four acres, was proposed to be built in Hayward. These facilities require substantial amounts of electricity. Its flat roof could be equipped with a photovoltaic system so that it could generate its own electricity and probably sell some back to the grid or to nearby buildings. State requirements and subsidies for solar installations would greatly increase the number of these installations.

The state should also continue to promote conservation because the market cannot. It is obvious that the market alone cannot promote energy efficiency, conservation, or alternative energy systems. It is truly not in the interests of energy companies to do so, as their primary interest is in promoting more consumption. Even "green" energy companies have this bias. While they can promote the use of renewable resources to generate electricity, they cannot compete effectively in the market—that is, generate profits—by encouraging their customers to use less electricity. Thus, it falls to government to develop policies and incentives that meet the collective interests of the public while energy companies produce what is needed to meet whatever demand there is.

For the states to protect their energy policy interests in a deregulated market, they must take a role in balancing the interests of both electricity providers and customers. Ironically, the states have a stronger role to play in a deregulated market to ensure that the market actually works as it is supposed to. To avoid the development of a real monopoly, the states must provide incentives for competitors to enter the market. This is the only way to ensure that consumers have real choices among providers. This could mean that the states will have to become electricity providers themselves if the market does not produce enough competition.

So states must guard against the possibility of market manipulation by designing deregulation policy that recognizes the weaknesses of the market model as well as its strengths and taking an active role in making sure it works the way it is advertised to do. Electricity *is not* pork bellies after all. It is a necessity of modern life that few, except the odd hermit, can choose to do without. The consequences of market manipulation do argue for some regulatory intervention in this marketplace.

Conclusion

It is clearly difficult to develop an even balance of the interests of both the market and the states. The market wants ever-higher profits while the states want to manage costs and protect the poor and the environment. The free market envisioned by economists cannot meet the states' multiple policy interests. Nor can the state support the excesses of the market and still meet the public's interests.

I have argued here that electricity policy must be designed in such a way that the states can achieve the public interest while enabling the market to do what it does best—provide a quality product. The deregulation policy that California adopted in 1996 did not achieve either of these goals. The state sacrificed all of its energy policy interests to a policy based on free market theory that serves individual but not collective interests. In the end, the companies' greed damaged their own long-term interests in California, leaving them with little credibility with the public or the government. The state has now developed organization structures and policies to guard against future market manipulations. Proposals to re-regulate are in the legislative works.

The greatest irony of all is that the experiment in free market electricity has resulted in a greater role for government at both the state and local levels in California than was ever considered in the first 100 years of the electricity industry. In 2001, California established new agencies to do the planning and demand-side management that used to be the job of the regulated industry. Local governments in California and elsewhere are looking into developing municipal electricity utilities and forming large buying cooperatives in order to negotiate better electricity prices. These are further evidence that the states put their other energy policy interests ahead of the market's promises for cheap electricity—promises that have failed to materialize almost everywhere.

To achieve a balance between market interests and the state's interests, policymakers must finally recognize the deficiencies of market theory when it comes to achieving public policy goals. This case clearly demonstrates that markets can produce wealth and even choice for some, but only government can guarantee that benefits will be available for everyone in the state.

10

The Future of Electricity Deregulation

The crisis in California had a significant impact on other states' restructuring activity. By February 2003, only eighteen states had completely deregulated, five had delayed restructuring, and one, California, had suspended deregulation. There was no active restructuring in more than half the states. Deregulation has ground to a screeching halt in all but those states that had been far along in the process before 2001. The states that are not active as of this writing include all of those in the Southeast and many in the Great Plains (see map in chapter 6).

This has led to a market that is more than half-regulated and only partially open to the market. Energy companies, on the other hand, have restructured and will continue to pressure the states in the interests of creating a national market that is completely deregulated. This chapter considers the aftermath of the California crisis as the truth about the companies' market manipulation unfolded, the impact of the "crisis in confidence" that developed in light of Enron's collapse, and the assurances that states will require before deregulation can again become a viable policy. I argue that the role of the Federal Energy Regulatory Commission (FERC) in the deregulated marketplace has changed with deregulation and that the FERC has become the dominant agency to protect the public's interests, not those of the industry. The future of the market and the states' policy needs in this market, whether or not the state has deregulated, are also discussed.

Aftermath of the Crisis

Before the end of the year 2001, Enron Corporation, the leading promoter of electricity restructuring, collapsed amid revelations of accounting practices that overstated company earnings. In the unfolding of Enron's story, there also came to light a series of memoranda that outlined trading schemes to manipulate the price of electricity on the California market. This was the smoking gun that lent credence to California's claims that market manipulation drove up the price of electricity during the winter of 2001. More evidence emerged that other electricity companies had withheld electricity from the market at the time to further reduce the supply and drive up prices. El Paso Corporation, a natural gas transmission company, also withheld gas from California further increasing the price of both gas and electricity (Oppel 2002). By early 2003, the FERC had found evidence that Enron and more than thirty other companies had manipulated prices during 2000–2001 and ruled that the state was entitled to refunds of $3.3 billion (Oppel 2003). The same report found that "Enron's online trading platform was 'a key enabler' of gas price manipulation."

The politics of these events has high significance. Kenneth Lay, Enron's former CEO, was in many ways the father of electricity deregulation. He was instrumental in persuading Congress and the first Bush administration to insert a clause in the Energy Policy Act of 1992 that allowed the development of exempt wholesale generators (EWGs) that could generate and sell electric power at wholesale without being subject to any regulatory restrictions at the national or state level. These entities did not exist at the time, but in a short while, Ken Lay refashioned Enron so that it would become the largest energy trading company in the country, an EWG that did not generate electricity itself but traded it, using emerging computer technology to buy excess electricity from one source and sell it to another. Lay thus developed the initial infrastructure that made electricity deregulation possible.

Lay then began to work to convince state legislators to restructure their electricity systems. He sought the support of then-Governor George W. Bush of Texas as he lobbied governors in other states to support deregulating their own utilities. When Governor Bush became President Bush, Lay and other energy company CEOs gained unprecedented access to the White House, especially because vice president Dick Cheney had been CEO of the Halliburton Company. The Vice President chaired a task force in the spring of 2001 to develop a new national energy policy. The task force's proceedings were kept secret from the public, but several large energy companies, including Enron, admitted to having had significant input into the proposed policy. No environmental groups were given the opportunity to sit on the task force. The draft energy policy that emerged was heavily biased toward energy development with little consideration of conservation as a national policy, a complete reversal of the energy policies of the 1970s and the 1992 policy. This proposed policy that favored market approaches to providing energy sufficiency for America was juxtaposed with the market focus of the Federal Energy Regulatory Commission at the same time. While Californians suffered blackouts because of market manipulation, the Republican majority in the federal government continued to argue that market forces alone would meet the nation's energy needs. As of February 2004, the energy policy had still not been adopted by Congress, despite Republican majorities in both houses of Congress.

The politics of the energy companies in the shadow of the California crisis may have led many states to approach deregulation more cautiously. Once it became more and more apparent that the companies had manipulated the California market, states slowed the process of restructuring until they could be assured that their other energy policy interests could be protected. In a deregulated market, the only assurance that states can have to protect their residents from predatory market practices must come from the national regulator, the FERC.

The 1992 Energy Policy Act elevated the role of federal watchdogs over state regulators as the move to restructure electricity in the states accelerated. Electricity deregulation or restructuring not only dismantles the state legal framework, which had developed over almost 100 years, but also limits the state's ability to protect other energy policy interests that are intertwined with regulation. Because state regulators in a free market lose their power to protect the public's multiple interests, federal regulators alone become responsible for ensuring that the market works fairly and efficiently.

The breakdown of the traditional federal-state regulatory partnership left California's citizens unprotected from predatory market practices that led to the highest retail electricity prices in the nation and drove a major public utility into bankruptcy. The case provides an example of the complex institutional impacts involved in implementing major new policy. It also raises questions about the federal role in regulating against bad policy design in the states and provides an illustration of the interplay of economics and politics within our federal system.

The Federal Energy Regulatory Commission's New Role[1]

Through the winter of 2001, while California scrambled to get control of the electricity market, this most important federal actor sat quietly on the sidelines. The FERC had been granted authority by the 1992 Energy Policy Act to ensure that wholesale electricity prices are "just and reasonable." Yet, even as wholesale electricity prices rose to unprecedented heights and the utilities were threatened with bankruptcy, the FERC refused to intervene in the California market. Had the FERC acted early to constrain wholesale prices, the state might have managed the crisis better with fewer political and economic consequences.

Market manipulation can easily occur in a market where the physical infrastructure of the industry limits the entrance of sellers into the marketplace. The fewer the suppliers in a market, the more power each will have to control how much product is made available on a daily basis and how high or low the price will be. We also know now that poor public policy can establish conditions that make market manipulation easier. In the political arena in which policy is developed, powerful industry voices often have the ability to design policies to maximize their own benefits, as happened in California.

For these reasons, it seems imperative that regulators at the state and federal levels maintain traditional regulatory roles that guard against predatory business practices that can distort the market's operations. In the case of electricity this includes the expectation that the FERC will step in to cap wholesale prices when they are clearly out of control. Had the FERC been willing to intervene in the California market in January 2001, the crisis might well have dissipated then. When the FERC finally did cap wholesale prices in late May, the market settled down and prices fell to more normal levels, even at the beginning of the summer, the period of peak electricity demand.

Throughout the winter and spring of 2000–2001, the state of California implored the FERC to place a cap on wholesale electricity prices in the western states. The FERC chairman, Curtis Hebert, with support from the George W. Bush administration, argued that capping prices would only reduce the supply of electricity available to the California market. The market was the solution not the problem, argued Hebert, despite the crippling effects of sky-high wholesale electricity prices on the state's residents and economy.

The crisis in California continued throughout the spring; state energy regulators predicted rolling blackouts all summer long; and the state's electricity deregulation program was suspended. Then, in May 2001, President Bush replaced Hebert as chair of the FERC with Patrick Wood III, a former Texas public utility commissioner. Within weeks of Wood's appointment, the FERC finally imposed a temporary price cap on wholesale electricity prices in the western states and ordered all western generators to sell their uncommitted power in the market. Contrary to economic theory, suppliers did not desert the market. By the end of June, wholesale electricity was selling for $100 per megawatt, down from $750 per megawatt the year before. Only later was it learned that without regulatory intervention, companies had deliberately withheld electricity from the California market in order to boost prices and their own profits.

The Federal Energy Regulatory Commission's Role in National Energy Policy

The Federal Energy Regulatory Commission was established in 1977 through the Public Utilities Regulatory Policy Act (PURPA) to regulate and oversee the interstate transmission and interstate wholesale sales of natural gas and electricity. It replaced the Federal Power Commission, retaining the responsibility for regulating wholesale energy prices in interstate commerce. One of its initial roles was to ensure that public utilities would accept electricity from small generators or qualifying facilities (QFs). Most of these QFs generated electricity through cogeneration or used other renewable resources. The FERC was also to ensure that wholesale prices of gas and electricity would be just and reasonable. A primary responsibility for the FERC at the time was to make sure that public utilities accepted electricity from QFs and to encourage them to think more seriously about generating electricity by using renewable resources.[2]

When deregulation of electricity became a reality with the passage of the 1992 Energy Policy Act, the FERC was designated as the coordinator for the EWGs to assist them in gaining access to utility-owned transmission lines. The FERC was also granted the power to determine reasonable prices for transmission services (Kreith and Burmeister 1993: 356). Thus, the agency that was designed in the 1970s to pressure utilities to accept electricity generated from renewable resources within the traditional regulatory structure became the protector of free market interests designed to dismantle the regulatory structure.

When states restructured their utilities and opened up their electricity markets, the determination of just and reasonable prices became a critical responsibility for the FERC. Under regulation, prices were developed using a "cost plus" method where the monopoly companies were granted the recovery of their production costs plus a reasonable profit. In a deregulated free market, economic theory assumes that prices will be determined through the dynamics of competition, supply, and demand. Just and reasonable prices, in theory, should be determined by whatever price the market will bear.

In 2001, under Chairman Hebert, the FERC was committed to the principle of free electricity markets, as were many leaders in the Bush administration, and opposed to price caps. Rather than stepping in to set prices, they supported the belief that, in time, the market itself would determine just and reasonable prices. According to Severen Borenstein, director of the University of California's Energy Institute in Berkeley, the FERCs market analysis at that time "amounted to religious faith in markets" (Lochhead 2002). Thus, the agency's unwillingness to step into the market might be seen as protecting the long-term interests of the state as it made the transition away from regulation in the short term if the market works the way it is supposed to.

Unfortunately, this may have encouraged the companies' predatory behavior. When the FERC finally did intervene in late spring, prices fell immediately. By sending a signal to the market that it was taking a stronger regulatory role, the FERC was able to rein in the companies' excesses.

The aftermath of the California experience with electricity deregulation and the revelations of market manipulation underscore the essential role of the federal government to moderate the free market and protect states' interests. This role was not contemplated when the FERC's responsibilities were expanded in 1992. A June 2002 study of FERC by the U.S. General Accounting Office (GAO) found that the agency was still not equipped to regulate and oversee energy markets.

The GAO found that the FERC did not have the authority to levy meaningful civil penalties and thus could not "pose a credible threat and deter anticompetitive behavior or violations of market rules by market participants" (U.S. General Accounting Office 2002: 5). The agency did not have an effective regulatory and oversight approach through which to determine if interstate wholesale prices are just and reasonable. It also lacked sufficient staff knowledgeable about competitive energy markets. After Patrick Wood took over as FERC chair in May 2001, the agency began working toward developing a stronger role as regulator. At the crucial time for California, however, the agency was largely unable to perform the kind of critical analysis needed to intervene in the market. The GAO documented that the FERC's strategic goals and objectives throughout the 1990s had focused more on market development than on market oversight. After Wood's arrival in the summer of 2001, the agency began to develop strategies to detect and regulate abuses of market power (U.S. GAO 2002: 36).

A major lesson from this case is that the FERC must now play a major role in ensuring that energy markets are working properly. The FERC's early inability to recognize the distortions in the California market damaged the credibility of the agency as well as public confidence in electricity restructuring as sound public policy. Wood agreed with the findings of the GAO report and revealed reorganization plans to detect market manipulation and "toughen enforcement as it continues to encourage a more open, but orderly, energy market" (Lochhead 2002).

Restoring the Federal-State Partnership

During the 1970s, the states and the federal government developed a partnership in energy policy that rested on a base of energy efficiency and conservation. That partnership was largely abandoned during the 1990s surge toward deregulation. The California case strongly suggests that states need federal partnership support to make deregulated markets work properly. When and under what circumstances the FERC should act are questions that go to the heart of intergovernmental relations in electricity policy. Should the FERC be expected to bail out states because of poor policy design? How quickly should the FERC intervene in a market that could balance itself out over time? At what point should national policy interests supersede market interests? The FERC's mission is both to promote competition in the electricity industry and to provide oversight in the public interest to guard against anticompetitive actions. The GAO found that the agency has been more successful in developing the market than in establishing effective oversight (U.S. GAO 2002: 35).

Electricity restructuring is still in the experimental stages at the state level. California policymakers designed the law under a set of assumptions that later proved to be flawed. During the crisis, the state was berated by pundits and electricity providers for the way its deregulation policy was designed. The Power Exchange (PX) was set up to buy the most expensive electricity on the market each day, which in itself encouraged "gaming" by the companies. This policy was designed to protect the interests of the state's utilities, which had lobbied for protection against too *low* prices in the market. Policymakers never imagined that this same mechanism would be an incentive to providers to raise prices to unprecedented levels. In the end, the PX proved to be the worst idea of all, a mechanism that enabled price gouging and encouraged the worst type of free market behavior.

The result of California's policy design was a distorted state market that also had national and international repercussions. Residents of Oregon, Washington, and British Columbia also faced price hikes as companies in those areas diverted electricity to the more lucrative California market. Companies in those states paid farmers to reduce their acreage of crops that use irrigation so that more electricity, generated by hydro, could be produced to sell to the market to the south. The attraction of windfall profits created shortages in these states, and this drove up their prices as well, although nowhere in the range of the prices in California. The FERC's action to cap wholesale prices was essential in bringing stability back to the western markets. Its inaction in January, ostensibly to allow the market to work as it is supposed to in theory actually encouraged the worst predatory market behavior.

With deregulation, electricity is now becoming a national market, no longer limited by state regulators. The national interest, therefore, is better served by ensuring that state restructuring policies are designed to enhance the effectiveness of the national market. A stronger FERC, focused on the public interest as well as the industry's, would work with the states to help design legislation that avoids the market distortions that occurred in California. The federal-state partnership in energy policy must be restored through a stronger FERC that provides effective oversight as well as promotes market development and works with the states to design effective policy. Such policy should include a mix of energy efficiency incentives as well as increased in-state supply to ensure that a state is not left to the mercies of a predatory market.

The States and the Future of the Market

While the FERC can become a strong force in ensuring that electricity markets work properly, no federal agency can meet the other state interests linked to energy policy. The state planning that characterized electricity regulation as a natural monopoly was discarded with deregulation. States that have deregulated are now less able to ensure that they will have a reliable supply of electricity at reasonable and predictable prices. All states now need to develop more comprehensive energy policies to guard against the predictable forces of the market. Such policies must include incentives and regulations to increase conservation and efficiency and the use of renewable, indigenous resources to generate electricity. State energy policies should also encourage the development of publicly owned electricity districts that are governed by the users—the citizens—who can determine what fuels are most desirable and acceptable[3] and can help keep market prices down. The vaunted simplicity of the market has introduced new complexity into state energy planning.

Can the Market Really Work to Protect the Public Interest?

The free marketers continue to promote energy deregulation as a long-term policy to supply the American demand for energy and to support domestic economic growth. At the same time, consumer product companies continue to supply the market with more new products that require energy to operate and thus drive up the demand for electricity. Americans' demand for energy increases with the market's production of energy-using items. The state's political need for low-priced energy is in conflict with the market's need for continual growth in that unlimited demand and limited supply will inevitably force prices to rise. The only way the states can avoid this reality is by developing policies that promote conservation, energy efficiency, and the use of renewable sources of energy.

States have to develop an understanding of how the market really works and decide whether it is the best way to achieve public policy goals. States restructured their electricity markets because they were convinced by economists and lobbyists representing large companies that competition would bring consumers provider choice and that choice would automatically lower prices. But in any market, it is fair to ask who gets the real choice. In the case of electricity, it is pretty clear that large users—factories, hotels, and shopping malls—get the best choices. They are able to contract directly with providers and negotiate the best prices. They were the strongest supporters of deregulation as a state policy in California and are the largest beneficiaries of the policy.

Retail and commercial customers do not get a real choice in the electricity market. While there may be choices, providers are still interested in maintaining at least a minimum price level and will abandon the market when that price level cannot be attained. This happened in Pennsylvania, where companies bailed out after the policy was implemented, and in Virginia, where they did not even enter the market because prices were already too low. Even when small customers do make a choice of supplier, they have no leverage over the market that determines monthly prices. They have no mechanism by which they can individually signal the market that the price is too high. They also have no pricing mechanism that gives them incentives to use energy at different times of the day when demand is greater or lower. Small customers are truly at the mercy of the market. Protecting their interests was one of the rationales for regulating utilities in the first place.

Big users can signal the market more easily by lessening demand to which the market responds by reducing supply. When demand picks up again, supply will naturally lag behind because it is no simple matter to drill new gas wells or restart an electricity generator. The "simple" law of supply and demand becomes problematic when producers reduce production in order to assure a high enough price to cover their costs and a reasonable profit. In energy production, the supply lags that lead to higher prices can cause ripples throughout the economy that can lead to inflation in a hot economy or slower recovery in a weak economy. Regulated energy markets had the capacity to even out economic cycles and pricing so that businesses and residential customers did not face widely varying prices of an essential commodity. Free market pricing of these goods prohibits businesses, families, governments, and nonprofit organizations from budgeting for energy costs with confidence. Low-income users in a market that diverges widely can be faced with hard choices between buying energy and other essentials. State energy policy has to consider how to protect low-income users from "unreasonable" energy prices. The state has to define what unreasonable means because the market considers that the only unreasonable price is the one that buyers will not pay. Where there are at least enough buyers to achieve energy producers' earnings goals, then prices can be defined as reasonable, even if 49 percent of the users cannot afford to pay.

The free marketers also promote deregulation as a means to spur innovation by unlocking the creative talents of unregulated companies. They assume, as a matter of dogma, that regulated companies have no incentive to be innovative because they are guaranteed a return on their investments. Yet if we examine electricity deregulation closely, it is difficult to see where the innovation is. It is certainly not in the production of electricity, which continues to be dependent on fossil fuels for most generation. Natural gas is the primary fuel for new power plants at the moment. The nuclear power industry is also trying to make a comeback, despite the lingering political dilemma of nuclear waste disposal in this country and new fears of terrorist attacks on nuclear power plants.

Regulated companies *were* slow in adopting renewable sources as fuels for electricity generation, and their decisions to build nuclear-powered generators raised the price of electricity as the cost of constructing and operating the plants rose. The regulated utilities were granted the authority to charge higher prices for this electricity and the amortization of these facilities is now a major issue for state deregulation policy. At the time these plants were constructed, however, the nuclear power industry was growing in prominence all over the world. France, for example, produces a high percentage of its electricity through nuclear power. In the United States, nuclear power has been controversial since its origins, and its opponents have picked up new support since the terrorists attacks of September 11, 2001, making it difficult to predict any shift away from natural gas to nuclear power in the short term.

Regulated companies were innovative, despite the assertions of market theorists. Companies knew that their requests for price increases would be whittled down to gain public support, so they looked for ways to reduce their operating costs. Many regulated utilities adopted demand-side management programs for their customers and themselves precisely because they profited from lowering demand. They had to develop new technologies to improve their own operating efficiency. The argument that regulated monopolies will not innovate does not stand up in the face of the evidence.

The major innovation from deregulation so far does not appear to be in creating new products to improve efficiency of electricity generation and transmission. It has been only in the buying and selling of electricity by adding a middleman and complexity to a relatively simple industry that worked pretty well for most consumers. It remains to be seen whether the unregulated market will produce innovation in electricity generation on its own. It is clear that the only way this can happen is if the companies are guaranteed a sufficient market share so that they can recoup their development costs and make a profit. This is unlikely to happen in a truly unfettered open market for electricity. It is far more likely for it to happen in an oligopoly where companies can guarantee their market share the way that regulated companies can. Prices will then be higher than they would be with more competition.

Pricing in the market is more complex than is typically presented by market theorists. The expectation that competition alone will drive down prices is overridden by the reality of an industry with high costs for development, both for the construction of power plants and the extraction of fuels, transmission, and distribution. The price of natural gas, which has been deregulated since the early 1980s, is determined by supply and demand. When the price of natural gas falls because of ample supply, however, companies stop drilling for new supplies because the market price is not high enough to assure them of cost recovery and a profit. As demand grows, then, prices must rise in order to provide the drillers with sufficient incentives to increase supply.

Most new electricity generating plants today are fueled by natural gas. Most new homes built in this country are fueled by either natural gas or electricity. Natural gas is desirable because it burns more cleanly than other fossil fuels, reducing the pollution. It does not take an expert, however, to predict that the demand for natural gas will rise in the foreseeable future, particularly when the U.S. economy recovers from the present recession. When that happens, the price of gas will inevitably rise and with it the price of electricity. States that deregulated for the promise of lower prices will find their prices higher and their residents and industries subject to the whims of a market that is interested only in its own profits to the detriment of the states' other energy policy interests.

The same market dynamic applies to power plant construction. California was criticized for not building new power plants during the 1990s. Yet, in the early years of the decade, the state was in the throes of an economic recession and demand for electricity was flat. When the deregulation legislation was enacted in 1996, there was a surplus of electricity in the western states and, thus, no demand for new power plants. At the height of the crisis, the state approved legislation to streamline the application process for new power plants (Senate Bill 28X). At least ten new power plants that were proposed in the summer of 2001 have now been delayed or put on hold because of the market slowdown (California Energy Commission 2003). The fact is that in a free market, companies do not invest in expensive generators in anticipation of market demand. That would only produce oversupply in an economic slowdown and further depress prices for their product. It takes a sustained economic boom with increasing demand to provide the incentives for companies to build new capacity.

U.S. policymakers at all levels should also reflect on the possible effects of increasing international energy demand from developing countries. Anyone who has traveled around the world, especially to developing countries like China, is struck by the desire of people in these countries to be like Americans. U.S. products and companies can be found everywhere. Kentucky Fried Chicken (KFC) has a store on the grounds of the Summer Palace in Beijing. I was told there that KFC is the most popular restaurant in the city. McDonald's does a roaring business in Moscow; in Sydney it sells McCapuccino. All over the developing world, billboards advertise American companies' products and the American lifestyle. School children in China are taught to speak English in the primary grades.

As the adoption of an American lifestyle grows throughout the world, so will the demand for the energy needed to support it. Logically, one has to conclude that the limited supply of fossil fuels on the planet will not be enough to go around. Can Americans assume that developing countries that currently have surplus energy resource supplies will continue to sell them to us instead of keeping them for their own use or selling them to another buyer? If prices rise to the point where only the rich can afford to buy, will there be political ramifications for the United States, both domestic and international?

The free market is in theory divorced from such political considerations. It is simply a mechanism by which products and services are exchanged for money according to supply and demand. It does not consider the moral or political questions of who benefits and who loses in these transactions and how one chooses without having equality of incomes. In a social and political world, where these questions matter, economic theory falls short and policymakers must consider how to protect the higher public policy values.

States now have a strong incentive to focus their efforts on encouraging efficiency and conservation in the short term and developing comprehensive energy policies for the longer term. To protect their energy policy interests, including reasonable prices for all users, states must identify their indigenous sources of renewable energy and provide incentives for the development of innovative technology. They should subsidize the use of solar and other technologies to encourage the development of personal electricity production. They should rewrite building codes to provide incentives for "green" construction and sustainable development. They should be wary of exposing their residents to the whims of the market and develop policies that provide protections to overcome market dynamics.

California adopted its new Energy Action Plan on May 8, 2003. Its stated goal is to:

> Ensure that adequate, reliable, and reasonably-priced electrical power and natural gas supplies, including prudent reserves, are achieved and provided through policies, strategies, and actions that are cost-effective and environmentally sound for California's consumers and taxpayers (State of California 2003: 2).

The new plan, developed in response to the 2001 electricity crisis, outlines the ways that the agencies will monitor the market, assure adequate supplies of energy, "protect the public's health and safety and ensure our quality of life." It also emphasizes protecting low-income populations from "disproportionate adverse impacts from the development of new energy systems" (State of California 2003: 3). The plan has six sets of actions: (1) Optimize Energy Conservation and Resource Efficiency; (2) Accelerate the State's Goal for Renewable Generation; (3) Ensure Reliable, Affordable Electricity Generation; (4) Upgrade and Expand the Electricity Transmission and Distribution Infrastructure; (5) Promote Customer and Utility Owned Distributed Generation; and (6) Ensure Reliable Supply of Reasonably Priced Natural Gas. The state will finance up to 300 megawatts of peaking capacity in critical areas to ensure local reliability and it will "implement a voluntary dynamic pricing system to reduce peak demand by as much as 1,500 to 2,000 megawatts by 2007" (State of California 2003: 5). The state has also accelerated the date by which renewable generation will constitute 20 percent of in-state capacity from 2017 to 2010.

California developed this plan in response to a crisis brought on by overreliance on a market that does not work under the same set of values that states do. This plan could have been developed earlier had the state understood the potential damages that could arise from enacting a deregulation policy that placed the state's energy consumers completely at the mercy of the market. Other states can learn from California's misfortunes and from what they now know about the market. The lesson is simple: protect your energy policy interests that are not shared by the energy industry. The market cannot deliver those policy interests.

11

Public Policy and the Market

The lessons from this case raise serious questions about whether the market is an effective mechanism for delivering public policy. Since the late 1970s, economists have argued that government inefficiencies hamper the effectiveness of the market economy. Regulation has been portrayed as the dead hand of government on the creativity and innovation of a free market freely operating.

This ideology has increasingly dominated political thinking about public policy and even about democracy and what it means to be an American. Libertarian politics put forth by various right-wing political think tanks (e.g., the Cato Institute) demand deregulation of the federal government and devolution of policymaking to the lowest governmental levels. The anarchy of the free market economy is portrayed as the ideal model for the political system, promoting individuality and eschewing both collective decisionmaking and true public interest. In this ideology, the ability of individuals to take care of themselves by getting what they can at the expense of their neighbors is the only public interest. That this translates into political anarchy instead of democratic collective policymaking seems not to disturb the ideologues.

The society that it creates is certainly not the one envisioned by the founders, even though they themselves were elites. What Alexis de Tocqueville[1] found in early America was a society based on "self-interest rightly understood," that is, understanding that individuals can be free only insofar as all others in the society are free. Public policy that results in undermining this concept does so at the expense of the very foundations of American democracy.

The great philosophers of economics, especially Adam Smith, saw economics as a system that could improve the lives of all people and the society. He mistrusted big government, but he also mistrusted big business and felt that government should moderate business activities so that they did not reduce competition (see Viner 1927). Smith wrote his thesis in eighteenth-century London, where the neighborhoods to this day are dotted with many small businesses that serve the needs and demands of their local customers. A market with lots of small businesses can meet individual needs that large businesses do not. Smith's thesis of perfect competition cannot be fulfilled in a market of giants that control essential information and manipulate consumer demand through advertising. Not even the Internet enables customers to have perfect information although it does improve the process.

The California case demonstrates the real hazard for government policymakers in depending on the market to deliver public policy for an essential commodity. Electricity is not just another commodity, after all, but a complex product the use of which is woven throughout the economy and public policy. When the price of electricity goes up, costs rise throughout the economy. Operating costs rise for businesses and governments, as well as for residents who pay the costs of home lighting, heating, and cooling. The costs of anything made from petrochemicals rises: plastics, fertilizers, drugs, and so forth. Costs of transportation rise, adding further to increases in commodity prices. Energy price increases contributed significantly to the inflation of the late 1970s. A commodity that has such a powerful impact on the whole economy, and one that users have few options not to use, cannot be equated to most other products in the market. Electricity production still has the markings of a natural monopoly, as Samuel Insull argued in the early 1900s.

Regulation assured the production of adequate supplies of electricity delivered at a price that was affordable for all consumers and produced in a way that protected a state's natural environment. These three public policy values have been associated with electricity policy for more than thirty years. Deregulation also unintentionally deregulates these related policies, as California and other states that deregulated discovered. When faced with out-of-control price increases and limited supplies of electricity, California stepped in immediately to protect these other energy policy interests and now has a much stronger role in governing energy production and delivery than it did before deregulation. Pressures in the state to reregulate cannot succeed because the utilities have been dismantled and, like Humpty Dumpty, cannot be put together again. But the state is taking serious steps to develop policies to ensure that it will never again be placed at the mercy of a voracious market.

From a broader perspective, this case also illustrates the challenge of making large institutional changes, especially when more than one level of government is involved. Electricity restructuring requires change in both state and federal institutions. This involves the creation of new sets of rules and procedures and a change in established ways of operating. Neither California nor the Federal Energy Regulatory Commission (FERC) was prepared to oversee a wildly out-of-control market. The state had to develop ways to intervene in the market, especially when the utilities were facing bankruptcy. The FERC did not have staff with the expertise to "monitor rapidly evolving energy markets" and to change "a dysfunctional organizational structure beset by frequent leadership changes" (Lochhead 2002: A1). California's new institutions, the Power Exchange and California Independent System Operator, operated efficiently but were ineffective, in part because of the policymakers' inability to foresee the potential for manipulation built into the policy design and in part because of the FERC's inability to analyze what was happening in the market. The FERC's emphasis at the time on protecting the interests of energy providers in a developing market undermined its own obligation to protect the interests of the public as defined in the 1978 law. Deregulation interrupts the federal-state partnership in energy policy that developed during the 1970s and extended through the early 1990s. Deregulation is seen as freeing the market from government interference, implying that no governmental partnership is needed. Without that partnership, however, the public interest is sacrificed to the interests of entrepreneurs whose principal focus is on improving their own bottom line. The public interest cannot be served without some government oversight of market practices. Thus, new policy initiatives can be hampered by old institutional arrangements that fail to adapt quickly enough to changing policy demands, particularly where agencies fail to focus on meeting the interests of the public as well as those of the industry.

The Proper Role of Government and the Proper Role of the Market

Governments considering adopting deregulation as a public policy also need to reflect on the proper role of government as well as the market. The government is a system for collective decisionmaking in the public interest. This concept gets lost in a market system simply because the market values individual choice more highly than it does collective choice or the public interest.

Governments that deregulate or privatize services can risk the loss of their capability to solve these problems except at great cost and more dislocation of resources—opportunity costs, to use an economics term. Once a service is privatized, a political lobby is established to ensure that more business will come the market's way. Witness, for example, the power of the prison industry in states where prisons have been privatized. In order to guarantee that cells will be filled, the industry lobbies for mandatory sentencing laws. Many states have learned that such laws tie the hands of judges and prosecutors and overcrowd prisons, placing higher demands on state budgets. So privatization does not reduce public budgets through all the supposed efficiency of the private sector. It creates demand for stronger policies and more budget resources to guarantee more business and higher earnings.

What is the proper role of the market in a democratic society? The great economists of the past saw economics as a way of improving society, not merely increasing the wealth of a few at the expense of many. Adam Smith's "invisible hand" was conceived as a way to achieve the maximum welfare for the whole society, so long as perfect competition governed the market's operations. Competition cannot be perfect in today's markets (if it ever existed outside of theory) nor are consumers equally qualified to participate in the market, thus it cannot be argued that maximum social welfare is ever really achieved.

The devotion of neoclassical economists to simple theories of market behavior becomes dogmatic in the face of the reality of the manipulation of the California electricity market. The response of reputable economists to the crisis was to call for a more free market and more deregulation, despite the obvious market manipulation that was occurring at the time. Any examination of energy demand during those months compared to previous years shouted that there was something very wrong with this market. It *had* to be manipulation, not just lower supplies because of the drought in Washington or bad policy design by California lawmakers. Most economists at the time refused to admit publicly that there could be anything wrong with the market. Nor would they recognize the serious consequences for the state from such high prices. The response to these concerns was that new markets take a while to stabilize, and, in the long term, prices would come down as supply and demand stabilized. Apparently, the interim would be the government's problem, while its own budget would be battered by higher operating costs and higher costs to subsidize small businesses and low-income residents in the state.

The dominant advocates of neoclassical economics fail to acknowledge that there should be a balance between the market and public policy. The mantra that the private sector can deliver government services better and at lower cost than government is fallacious in many instances. Economists and neoconservative policymakers rarely, if ever, ask who really benefits and who really pays for public policy. Political rhetoric misleads the public into believing that benefits are more widespread than they truly are. Government-bashing has become de rigueur for politicians of both parties. The bureaucracy is seen as the problem not the solution and the only way to solve public problems is to turn them over to the private sector. Yet precious little evidence has been provided to justify these conclusions.

Since the early days of public administration, governments have striven to follow private sector norms for management and policy development. Government at all levels is arguably more business-like than ever before. At the same time, citizen alienation toward government is also greater than ever before, leading some to question whether these practices themselves have distanced government from the people they are supposed to be serving (King and Stivers 1998).

I have tried to demonstrate here that government has a critical role to play in making our society and our economy work. The lesson from the California case is simple: When one policy is turned over to the market, governments lose control of all the other policy interests that are connected to it. Deregulation or privatization is not simple, then, and policymakers must approach it with a clear understanding of all the interconnected policy interests involved and what they are trading off. Policymakers must also accept their role to protect the public interest and recognize that the private sector cannot do this job. Deregulation of essential commodities or the achievement of public goals abdicates governmental responsibility and abandons the public interest to an institution that simply cannot achieve it. It is now time for government to be government and let the market be the market.

The future of electricity restructuring is murky at best. Fewer than half the states have deregulated their markets while the industry itself has moved quickly to restructure under the provisions of the 1992 Energy Policy Act. Given this divide between public policy interests in the

147

states and private interests in the market, we can expect increasing pressure on the states to deregulate so that the market can work efficiently. States are wary now, however, and many of those that did deregulate have had second thoughts. The trend toward increased government involvement in electricity markets should continue through new municipal power production, incentives for renewable resource generation and personal power generation, and municipal buying cooperatives as in Ohio and Massachusetts.

State governments must also read their own energy policy mission statements and identify ways to protect the policy interests that are explicitly interconnected before developing any policy to deregulate electricity. The evidence is clear that the states have had a complex of policy interests related to energy across thirty years. California and many other states were persuaded to deregulate electricity by the promise of low prices to serve the interests of their residents and businesses. Those promises were not and could not be fulfilled and the state moved finally to protect the complex of policy interests. Other states should move carefully to deregulate, armed with an understanding of what they are giving up and how they can maintain control over those other values that matter.

In the end, it is government that must serve the people's interests and not the market. Government may be slow to innovate and messy, but that is the way American democracy is structured. Economists emphasize efficiency as the highest value and advocate privatization as the way to increase efficiency in the government. Yet we ought to question whether efficiency is the most important value for public policy when it disadvantages the powerless and leads to public alienation of government. In any case, the word "efficiency" does not appear anywhere in the U.S. Constitution, so we should conclude that the messy structure the founders established was not intended to be efficient. It was intended to serve the people, all the people, and not just to protect the interests of a free market economy, which is not mentioned in the document either.

The fallacy of today's economic theory is the assumption that free markets alone can serve the interests of all the people. This case demonstrates that markets reward the cleverest and most powerful. Only governments can protect and serve the public.

12

Epilogue

On August 14, 2003, as I was putting the finishing touches on this manuscript, the electricity went out throughout much of the northeastern part of the United States and southeastern Canada. The great blackout of 2003 was the most extensive in North American history.

While reports are still preliminary, they do indicate that deregulation may lie at the base of the blackout insofar as it disrupted the management of the electricity grid that was in place under regulation. In Ohio, where the blackout started, companies in the north and south of the state are connected to two different independent system operators (ISOs) that did not communicate with each other about the extent of outages in their systems. This lack of communication led the companies to demand more electricity from a grid that was already overloaded. Like dominoes falling, each state's demand put more and more pressure on the entire grid until it shut down everywhere from New York to Michigan and north to Ontario and New England.

Deregulation disrupted communications among competing companies while it also linked them all to the transmission grid. When one company needed power, it took it from another part of the interlocked grid. Because none of the ISOs knew the full extent of the problem, they could not react fast enough to stop the cascading effect of the failures. So Ohio pulled on power supplies in Michigan, which pulled on Ontario, which then pulled on New York, and the lights went out everywhere for as long as twenty-four hours in some places (Lipton, Perez-Pena, and Wald 2003).

The blackout was also blamed on the aging transmission grid that is not capable of carrying the electricity demanded by the new markets. Electricity demand grows with the economy as we have already seen. It may grow at faster rates with deregulation, however, because competition leads all companies to encourage consumers to use more of their

149

product. Without regulatory efforts to encourage energy efficiency and conservation, demand for electricity will grow, putting more pressure on the grid.

Under the regulated monopoly model, the electricity providers (independently owned utilities) owned the grids and upgraded them as demand grew. They were required to use integrated resource planning and demand-side management programs to control growth in demand and resulting pressure on the grid. The companies that sold electricity also managed the grid and had the incentive to make sure that there was enough capacity to carry their own electricity to their customers. Deregulation removes responsibility for the grid from the profit-making providers and leaves it in the hands of the local companies that can no longer manage it. No one has the incentive to invest in upgrading the grid because the profitmakers use any grid to get their product to the area with the most demand. The federal government is now facing the prospect of investing billions to expand the electricity grid nationwide so that private companies can sell more electricity.

This crisis has not yet brought Americans to discuss the implications of ever-expanding electricity demand on our environment and our pocketbooks. If we continue to build more and more conventional power plants and bigger and bigger grids, the impact on our environmental heritage will surely be severe. It will take a bigger crisis to convince Americans that energy efficiency and alternative sources of energy are the only way to ensure that there will be enough to go around. Californians learned this lesson in 2001, although it did not last. As soon as prices stabilized and people got used to paying more for electricity, demand started to rise. Figure 12.1 illustrates the impact that the 2001 conservation efforts would have had on the 2002 peak demand.

The American Council for an Energy-Efficient Economy found that energy efficiency programs in California, New York, and New England reduced peak demand by more than 4,300 megawatts in 2001, which is the equivalent of about fifteen medium-sized power plants (www.aceee.org and www.eren.doe.gov).

Until Americans realize that unlimited demand for electricity leads only to more demand, we can expect more blackouts and higher prices for electricity and everything that is related to it. There is no free lunch when it comes to energy. While regulation was designed to manage electricity growth and profits, deregulation leads to an out-of-control market that will increase demand exponentially. Inevitably, more demand

Figure 12.1 **Peak Electricity Demand in the Independent System Operator Control Area** (on July 10, 2002, with available resources and alternative demand scenarios)

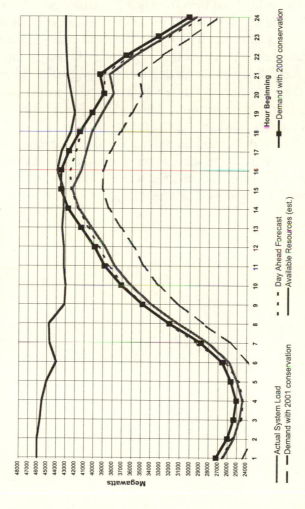

Source: California Energy Commission Web site: www.energy.ca.gov/electricity/peak_demand/2002-07-10_CHART.PDF.

Notes: This graph compares the July 10, 2002 demand with two alternative scenarios. The top line shows the available electricity generation resources on that day. Rolling blackouts typically would occur when operating reserves dip below 2 percent. The dotted line is the ISO's forecast of expected demand, which closely parallels the line that shows the actual demand in the ISO control area. The dashed line on the bottom illustrates the Energy Commission's scenario of what demand could have been if Californians were conserving at the same rate as the summer of 2001. The black line represents what electricity demand would have been based on 2000 usage patterns.

means that prices will rise as supplies of natural gas, the current fuel of choice for electricity generation, start to decline.

The blackout and the California electricity crisis underscore the need for a comprehensive look not only at energy policy in this country but at ways that ordinary Americans can provide more of their own energy. Given today's technology and the efficiency of smaller generators, it is time to look beyond the delivery of electricity using early twentieth-century technology such as fossil fuel generation and transmission grids. Deregulation has created a market that is going in the wrong direction by increasing dependency on outmoded technology. States and energy users need to think more creatively about generating smaller amounts of electricity closer to the end users. This would reduce traffic on the grid and avoid massive blackouts in the future.

I hope that I have demonstrated adequately the weaknesses of the market for delivering public policy. Both of these crises demonstrate the value of government involvement in a market that is truly a public good. Electricity is not pork bellies after all.

Appendix 1

State Energy Offices and Web Sites

State	State energy office	Energy office Web site
Alabama	Department of Economic and Community Affairs, Science, Technology and Energy Division	http://adeca.state.al.us/adeca/pages/pages_stm/Science_Technology_Energy_STE.stm
Alaska	Community and Economic Development, Alaska Industrial Development and Export Authority, Alaska Energy Authority	www.aidea.org/aea.htm
	Research and Rural Development Division Division, Alaska Housing Finance Corporation	www.ahfc.state.ak.us/
Arizona	Department of Commerce, Energy Office	www.azcommerce.com/energy.htm
Arkansas	Arkansas Industrial Development Commission, Arkansas Energy Office	www.aedc.state.ar.us/energy/
California	California Energy Commission	www.energy.ca.gov/
Colorado	Colorado Governor's Office of Energy Management and Conservation	www.state.co.us/oemc/
Connecticut	Connecticut Office of Policy and Management, Policy Development and Planning—Energy	www.opm.state.ct.us/aboutopm.htm
Delaware	Division of Facilities Management Energy Office	www.delaware-energy.com

(continued)

Appendix 1 *(continued)*

State	State energy office	Energy office Web site
Florida	Florida Department of Community Affairs	www.dca.state.fl.us/index.htm
Georgia	Georgia Environmental Facilities Authority, Division of Energy Resources	www.gefa.org/energy_program.html
Hawaii	Department of Business, Economic Development and Tourism, Energy Resources and Technology Division	www.hawaii.gov/dbedt/ert/energy.html
Idaho	Idaho Department of Water Resources, Energy Division	www.idwr.state.id.us/energy/
Illinois	Illinois Department of Commerce and Community Affairs, Bureau of Energy and Recycling	www.commerce.state.il.us/aboutdcca/
Indiana	Indiana Department of Commerce, Energy Policy Division	www.state.in.us/doc/energy/
Iowa	Iowa Department of Natural Resources, Energy and Geological Resources Division, Energy Bureau	www.state.ia.us/dnr/energy/
Kansas	Kansas Corporation Commission, Energy Programs Section	www.kcc.state.ks.us/energy/index.htm
Kentucky	Kentucky Division of Energy	www.nr.state.ky.us/nrepc/dnr/energy/dnrdoe.html
Louisiana	Louisiana Department of Natural Resources, Technology Assessment Division, Energy Section	www.dnr.state.la.us/SEC/EXECDIV/TECHASMT/ENERGY/IntroFrame.htm

Maine	Maine Department of Economic and Community Affairs Development, Energy Conservation Division	www.state.me.us/spo/
Maryland	Maryland Energy Administration	www.energy.state.md.us/
Massachusetts	Massachusetts Department of Economic Development, Division of Energy Resources	www.state.ma.us/doer/
Michigan	Michigan Department of Consumer and Industry Services, Energy Office	www.cis.state.mi.us/opla/erd/
Minnesota	Minnesota Department of Commerce, Energy Division	www.commerce.state.mn.us/pages/EnergyMain.htm
Mississippi	Mississippi Development Authority, Energy Division	www.decd.state.ms.us/main/energy/
Missouri	Department of Natural Resources, Energy Center	www.dnr.state.mo.us/de/homede.htm
Montana	Montana Department of Environmental Quality	www.deq.state.mt.us/energy/
Nebraska	Nebraska State Energy Office	www.nol.org/home/NEO/
Nevada	Nevada Department of Business and Industry, State Energy Office	http://energy.state.nv.us/
New Hampshire	Governor's Office of Energy and Community Services	www.state.nh.us/governor/energycomm/index.html
New Jersey	New Jersey Board of Public Utilities, Division of Energy	www.bpu.state.nj.us/wwwroot/energy/energy.htm
New Mexico	New Mexico Energy, Minerals and Natural Resources Department, Energy Conservation and Management Division	www.emnrd.state.nm.us/ecmd/

(continued)

155

Appendix 1 *(continued)*

State	State energy office	Energy office Web site
New York	New York State Energy Research and Development Authority	www.nyserda.org/
North Carolina	North Carolina Department of Administration, State Energy Office	www.doa.state.nc.us/doa/energy/energy.htm
North Dakota	North Dakota Division of Community Services, Energy Programs	www.state.nd.us/dcs/Energy/default.html
Ohio	Ohio Department of Development, Office of Energy Efficiency	www.odod.state.oh.us/cdd/oee/
Oklahoma	Oklahoma Department of Commerce, Division of Community Affairs and Development	www.odoc.state.ok.us/index.html
Oregon	Oregon Office of Energy	www.energy.state.or.us/
Pennsylvania	Pennsylvania Department of Environmental Protection, Office of Pollution and Compliance Assistance	www.dep.state.pa.us/dep/deputate/pollprev/pollution_prevention.html
Rhode Island	Rhode Island State Energy Office	www.riseo.state.ri.us/
South Carolina	South Carolina Energy Office	www.state.sc.us/energy/
South Dakota	South Dakota Governor's Office of Economic Development	www.sdgreatprofits.com/

Tennessee	Tennessee Department of Economics and Community Development, Energy Division	www.state.tn.us/ecd/energy.htm
Texas	Texas Comptroller of Public Accounts, State Energy Conservation Office	www.seco.cpa.state.tx.us/
Utah	Utah Energy Office	www.dced.state.ut.us/energy/
Vermont	Vermont Department of Public Service, Energy Efficiency Division	www.state.vt.us/psd/ee/ee.htm
Virginia	Virginia Department of Mines, Minerals and Energy, Division of Energy	www.mme.state.va.us/de/
Washington	Washington Department of Community, Trade and Economic Development, Energy Policy Office	www.energy.cted.wa.gov/
West Virginia	West Virginia Development Office, Energy Efficiency Program	www.wvdo.org/community/eep.htm
Wisconsin	Wisconsin Department of Administration, Division of Energy and Public Benefits, Energy Bureau	www.doa.state.wi.us/depb/boe/index.asp
Wyoming	Wyoming Business Council, Energy Program	www.wyomingbusiness.org/wbc/internal.cfm?areaID=1&navDetailID=176

Appendix 2

Priority Areas

Priority area	States	Total
Alternative energy development (biomass, fuel cells, solar, tidal energy, ethanol, methane, wind, photovoltaic)	Alabama, Alaska, Arizona, California, Colorado, Delaware, Hawaii, Idaho, Illinois, Indiana, Iowa, Kansas, Kentucky, Louisiana, Maryland, Massachusetts, Michigan, Minnesota, Montana, Nebraska, Nevada, New Jersey, North Carolina, North Dakota, Oregon, Pennsylvania, Rhode Island, South Carolina, Tennessee, Texas, Utah, Vermont, Virginia, Washington	34
Consumer tips on energy efficiency including home energy and appliance rating; energy rebates	Alaska, Arizona, California, Delaware, Georgia, Illinois, Indiana, Iowa, Kansas, Kentucky, Massachusetts, Michigan, Minnesota, Montana, Nevada, New Hampshire, New Jersey, New York, Ohio, Oklahoma, Oregon, Rhode Island, South Carolina, Texas, Utah, Vermont, Virginia, Washington, Wisconsin	29
Transit programs (carpooling, vanpooling, ridesharing, fleets containing alternative fuel vehicles)	Alabama, California, Delaware, Georgia, Hawaii, Indiana, Iowa, Kentucky, Louisiana, Maryland, Massachusetts, Michigan, Minnesota, Mississippi, Missouri, Nebraska, New Jersey, New Mexico, North Carolina, Ohio, Oklahoma, Rhode Island, South Carolina, Tennessee, Utah	26
Technical assistance and energy audits of residential and commercial buildings and schools; "institutional conservation programs"	California, Idaho, Illinois, Iowa, Kentucky, Louisiana, Maryland, Massachusetts, Michigan, Mississippi, Missouri, New Hampshire, North Carolina, Ohio, Oklahoma, Oregon, Pennsylvania, Rhode Island, South Carolina, Tennessee, Texas, Washington, Wisconsin	23
Energy tax credits, low interest loans, grants or bonds for upgrades of residential and commercial buildings and schools	Alabama, Alaska, Arizona, California, Colorado, Hawaii, Indiana, Iowa, Louisiana, Maryland, Massachusetts, Michigan, Mississippi, Montana, Nebraska, North Carolina, Ohio, Oregon, South Carolina, Wyoming	20

(continued)

159

Appendix 2 *(continued)*

Priority area	States	Total
Residential and commercial energy efficiency codes, standards	Alabama, Alaska, California, Colorado, Delaware, Hawaii, Illinois, Kansas, Kentucky, Louisiana, New Mexico, North Carolina, North Dakota, Oklahoma, Oregon, Pennsylvania, Rhode Island, Texas, Vermont	19
Governmental buildings/state facilities programs	Delaware, Iowa, Kentucky, Massachusetts, Mississippi, Missouri, Montana, Nebraska, New Hampshire, New Mexico, North Dakota, Oklahoma, Rhode Island, South Carolina, Texas, Utah	16
Weatherization assistance for low-income residents; fuel assistance	Alaska, Arizona, Colorado, Georgia, Nebraska, New Hampshire, North Dakota, Ohio, Oregon, Rhode Island, Vermont, Wisconsin	12
Recycling programs	Alabama, Colorado, Connecticut, Hawaii, Illinois, Indiana, Montana, Utah, Washington	9
Energy education programs to primary and secondary schools	Delaware, Georgia, Ohio, South Carolina, Tennessee, Texas, Utah, Wyoming	8
Statistics on state energy usage	California, Delaware, Georgia, Hawaii, Kentucky, Massachusetts, Minnesota, North Dakota	8
Water resources management/water quality issues	California, Colorado, Connecticut, Florida, Louisiana, Montana, Pennsylvania, Rhode Island	8
Emergency contingency planning (petroleum)	Alaska, California, Delaware, Hawaii, Rhode Island, Tennessee, Washington	7
Teaming with a university to undertake a special energy project	Alabama, Delaware, Georgia, Maryland, North Carolina, South Carolina, Washington	7

Treatment, storage, disposal of low-level radioactive waste; brownfields cleanup	Connecticut, Florida, Hawaii, New York, Oregon, South Carolina, Texas	7
Air resources management/air quality issues	Connecticut, Delaware, Florida, Indiana, Montana, Oklahoma	6
Climate change action	California, Hawaii, Oregon, New Mexico, South Carolina, Tennessee	6
Industry-specific energy efficiency programs	Alaska (fishing), Florida (cruise ships), Iowa (agriculture), North Carolina (agriculture), Vermont (agriculture), Washington (glass, wood)	6
Software packages enabling municipalities to track energy use and costs or policy scenario analysis	Arizona, Hawaii, Michigan, Vermont, Virginia, Washington	6
Regulatory and legislative coordination around energy issues	Connecticut, Delaware, Hawaii, Maine, Washington	5
Training energy management personnel to monitor or control energy consumption	Hawaii, Mississippi, Tennessee, Texas, Wyoming	5
Municipal solid waste management programs: sewer/wastewater management/groundwater issues	Alabama, California, Connecticut	3
Sustainable development/smart growth initiatives	Colorado, Georgia, Utah	3
Powerplants and licensing	California, New York	2
Technical assistance for businesses starting telework programs (telecommuting)	Oregon, Washington	2

Notes

Notes to Chapter 1

1. For a history of national policy, see Nash (1968).

2. A barrel of oil is the standard measure used to describe quantities of energy regardless of the fuel.

3. The United States still lags behind the rest of the world in public transportation. Nonetheless, several major public transportation systems were constructed in the 1970s, including the Washington, DC Metro and the San Francisco Bay Area Rapid Transit.

4. State energy policy has been focused on electricity, natural gas, and heating oil because states have no authority over transportation fuel policy.

Notes to Chapter 2

1. A building of this vintage in the city of Pittsburgh had an HVAC system that was designed to operate air conditioning and steam heating simultaneously the year around. An energy audit in 1980 indicated that the city could save $100,000 per year for an investment of $200,000 to upgrade the system.

2. In 1980, Aramco became 100 percent Saudi owned, with the date of ownership backdated to 1976 (www.saudinf.com).

3. It is hard to remember, given the politics of the past twenty years, that environmental protection was a highly salient political issue in the early 1970s. Environmental legislation passed both houses of Congress by huge majorities and virtually every candidate for political office in the country, even conservative Republicans, had a position statement favoring environmental protection.

4. Gasoline prices today, if adjusted for inflation, are approximately equivalent to 1973's pre-embargo price of 25 cents per gallon.

5. Clinton's vice president, Al Gore, had proposed, in his book *Earth in the Balance,* such a tax at 50 cents to reduce gasoline consumption. During the 1992 campaign, Reform Party candidate Ross Perot had educated Americans about the deficit and proposed a gasoline tax to eliminate it.

6. Refiners in California justify the higher prices by the fact that refineries have to produce a specialized mix to meet California air quality standards. Prices vary considerably in the state, however, with the highest prices seen in the San Francisco area.

7. The vice president claimed executive privilege in refusing to release the names and proceedings of the task force. The General Accounting Office sued the Executive Branch for release of this information. The case was still pending as this manuscript was completed.

Notes to Chapter 3

1. The 1977 amendments permitted California to impose higher standards on cars sold within the state. The manufacturers accepted this requirement because of the large market in California.

2. Historically, federal energy policy has always been linked with national security. The first energy "crisis" occurred during World War I when oil shortages threatened the war effort. The U.S. government established what was later to become the National Petroleum Institute (see Nash 1968).

3. The project was funded through the National Institute for Global Environmental Change, Midwestern Center, Indiana University, Bloomington.

4. The mid-continent states have blistering hot and humid summers as well as very cold winters. Thus, their air-conditioning demand and winter fuel needs are both high.

5. Ohio, not a respondent to the survey, was developing a state energy policy at the time. The policy was unveiled in 1994.

6. The Indiana legislature had no energy or environment committee. I was referred instead to the chief lobbyist for the electricity industry.

Notes to Chapter 4

1. The future of nuclear power is still uncertain. The industry continues to tout it as cheap, safe, and nonpolluting. Since the terrorist attacks on September 11, 2001, however, existing nuclear power plants are increasingly seen as a potential target and a major source of risk for residents near them.

2. Green Mountain Energy moved into the California market and quickly enrolled a sizable number of customers. I asked the sales rep what they were doing to encourage conservation. He could tell me only that they were able to build new power plants using renewables. He also said that they do, of course, encourage people to conserve energy.

Notes to Chapter 5

1. For an explanation of stranded costs, see chapter 4.

2. Because natural gas had been deregulated in the 1980s, residential prices for gas used for heating and cooking were already being passed along to customers.

3. In September of that year, my husband and I replaced our major kitchen appliances and furnace. At the time, there were no public urgings to buy the most efficient units. There was no public report of excess demand for electricity in the state.

4. Data from the California Energy Commission; available at: www.energy. ca.gov/electricity/monthly_off_line.html.

5. In June 2003, the FERC ruled that the contracts should stand even though it found that the companies acted to drive up prices (FERC 2003).

Notes to Chapter 7

1. Research for this chapter was performed by Rachel Levine, MPA student at California State University, Hayward. She also wrote a substantial part of the chapter.

2. To be sure, electricity was not the principal reason for the economic decline in 2001, but it may have been a contributing factor. Following the recession, the number of businesses that move to states with lower rates will provide a truer test of the effects of electricity restructuring.

Notes to Chapter 8

1. In this context, State refers to government in general as distinct from the states.

2. The Interstate Commerce Commission, established in 1880, was the first regulatory agency. It was disestablished during the 1990s.

3. Some will argue that these two groups are the same. At the time this manuscript was being prepared, the General Accounting Office had sued the president to release the names of task force members because their work was done in secret.

4. The credit business is very successful among those with the least financial resources. Many college students are enticed into taking on credit debt by companies that are permitted to solicit on campus.

5. Mishandling the energy crisis was one of the reasons Californians recalled Governor Gray Davis in October 2003.

Notes to Chapter 10

1. Portions of this section appeared in Timney (2002).

2. Interview with former congressman Richard Ottinger, cosponsor of PURPA.

3. The Sacramento Municipal Utilities District closed a nuclear power plant after citizens voted to pay higher rates to amortize the cots of removing the plant.

Note to Chapter 11

1. Alexis de Toqueville was an aristocratic Frenchman who came to the United States in 1831 to study democracy as a new form of government. His two-volume work, *Democracy in America*, remains a seminal description of early nineteenth century American culture and governance.

References

Bailey, Mary Timney. 1984. "Improving Energy Management and Accountability in Municipal Operations: A Model Energy Budget for Local Governments." Report of the Energy Task Force of the Urban Consortium for Technology Initiatives. Washington, DC: Public Technology, Inc.

————. 1993. "Energy Policy Development in the States: Implications for Global Warming Policy." Project report prepared for the National Institute for Global Environmental Change. Bloomington: Indiana University, Midwestern Center.

Banerjee, Neela, and Richard Pérez-Pena. 2001. "A Failed Energy Plan Catches Up to New York." *New York Times*, June 1: A1, A20.

"A Blinkered Strategy." 2001. *New York Times*, May 6: 14.

Brennan, Timothy J.; Karen L. Palmer; and Salvador A. Martinez. 2002. *Alternating Currents: Electricity Markets and Public Policy.* Washington, DC: Resources for the Future.

Brennan, Timothy J.; Karen L. Palmer; Raymond J. Kopp; Alan J. Krupnick; Vito Stagliano; and Dallas Burtraw. 1996. *A Shock to the System: Restructuring America's Electricity Industry.* Washington, DC: Resources for the Future.

Brower, Michael C.; Michael W. Tennis; Eric W. Denzler; and Mark M. Kaplan. 1993. *Powering the Midwest: Renewable Electricity for the Economy and the Environment.* Washington, DC: Union of Concerned Scientists.

California Energy Commission. 2003. Energy Facility Status, May 21; available at: www.ca.gov/sitingcases/all_projects.xls.

Davis, David Howard. 1978. *Energy Politics.* New York: St. Martin's Press.

————. 2001. "The Energy Crisis of 2001." Paper presented at the annual conference of the American Society for Public Administration, Newark, NJ, March 11.

Davis, Peter V. 1983. "Selling Saved Energy: A New Role for the Utilities." In *Uncertain Power: The Struggle for a National Energy Policy*, ed. Dorothy S. Zinberg, 182–98. Elmsford, NY: Pergamon Press.

Douglass, Elizabeth. 2003. "El Paso Pledges to Aid Probes of Other Firms." *Los Angeles Times*, March 22: C2.

Energy Information Administration. 2000. "The Restructuring of the Electric Power Industry," January; available at: www.eia.doe.gov/cneaf/electricity/page/restructure.html.

————. 2002. Annual Energy Review; available at: www.eia.gov/emeu/aer/pdf/pages/sec8.pdf.

————. 2003. "Status of State Electric Restructuring Activity," February; available at: www.eia.gov/cneaf/electricity/chg_str/regmap.html.

Federal Energy Regulatory Commission. 2003. "Commission Upholds Western Power Contracts, Connecticut Contract." News Release, June 25; available at: www.ferc.gov.

Foster Electric Report. 2002. "Study by Consumer Group Finds That Restructuring of Electric and Natural Gas Industries Has Been Harming Residential Customers." Report No. 274. September 25: 10ff.

Gaudette, Karen. 2001. "State Offers Electricity Bargains." *Hayward Daily Review,* NEWS, July 19: 1, 9.

Geissenger, Steve. 2001. "California Cringes at Power Deal." *Hayward Daily Review,* NEWS, June 2: 1, 7.

Gore, Al. 1991. *Earth in the Balance: Ecology and the Human Spirit.* New York: Houghton Mifflin.

Gornstein, Leslie. 2001. "California Power Use Plummets." *Hayward Daily Review,* July 2: 1, 7.

Harden, Blaine. 2001. "River's Power Aids California and Enriches the Northwest." *New York Times,* May 1: A1, A18.

Johnson, Kirk. 2000. "Feeling Powerless in a World of Greater Choice; Consumers Grow More Anxious As They Are Cut Loose in Electricity's New Free Market." *New York Times,* August 27: Sec. 1, 29.

————. 2001. "New York Turns Into a Lab on the Future of Electricity." *New York Times,* July 25: A1, A17.

Joskow, Paul L. 1975. "Applying Economic Principles to Public Utility Rate Structures: The Case of Electricity." In *Studies in Electric Utility Regulation,* ed. Charles J. Cicchetti and John L. Jurewitz, 17–72. Cambridge, MA: Ballinger.

Kahn, Joseph. 2002. "Californians Call Enron Documents the Smoking Gun." *New York Times,* May 8: A1, C6.

Kash, Don E., and Robert W. Rycroft. 1984. *U.S. Energy Policy: Crisis and Complacency.* Norman: University of Oklahoma Press.

Kraul, Chris. 1996. "Radical Changes in Power Industry Pass Legislature." *Los Angeles Times,* September 1: A1.

Kreith, Frank, and George Burmeister. 1993. *Energy Management & Conservation.* Denver: National Conference of State Legislatures.

Krugman, Paul. 2001. "Turning California On." *New York Times,* June 27: A25.

Lay, Kenneth. 2001. "Generating Ideas: Deregulation, Done Right This Time—Not State Control—Is the Answer to California's Energy Woes." *San Francisco Chronicle,* March 1: A23.

Lazarus, David. 2001. "Enron's Chief Denies Role as Energy Villain." *San Francisco Chronicle,* March 4: A1.

Lee, Henry. 1983. "National Energy Policy From State and Local Perspectives." In *Uncertain Power: The Struggle for a National Energy Policy,* ed. Dorothy S. Zinberg, 157–181. Elmsford, NY: Pergamon Press.

Lipton, Eric; Richard Pérez-Pena; and Matthew L. Wald. 2003. "Overseers Missed Big Picture as Failures Led to Blackout." *New York Times,* September 13: 1.

Lochhead, Carolyn. 2002. "Energy Regulator Says Agency's Inept." *San Francisco Chronicle,* June 19: A1, A10.

Lowe, Benjamin Y. 2002. "Pennsylvania, New Jersey Receive No Savings from Power Competition." *Philadelphia Inquirer,* May 20: A1, ff.

Meadows, Donella H.; Dennis L. Meadows; Jorgen Randers; and William H. Behrens III. 1972. *The Limits to Growth: A Report for the Club of Rome's Project on the Predicament of Mankind.* New York: Universe.

Mitchell, Eve. 2001. "PUC Expected to Accept New Plan." *Hayward Daily Review,* September 20: Business, 1, 5.

Nash, Gerald D. 1968. *United States Oil Policy 1890–1964.* Pittsburgh: University of Pittsburgh Press.

Olson, Mancur Jr. 1965. *The Logic of Collective Action: Public Goods and the Theory of Groups.* Cambridge, MA: Harvard University Press.

Oppel, Richard A. Jr. 2001. "Surplus of Finger-Pointing in California Energy Crisis." *New York Times,* June 5: A1, C2.

———. 2003. "Panel Finds Manipulation by Energy Companies." *New York Times,* March 27: A14.

Oppel, Richard A. Jr. with Lowell Bergman. 2002. "Judge Says Supplier Inflated Gas Prices in California Crisis." *New York Times,* September 24: A1, C2.

Oppel, Richard A. Jr., and Laura M. Holson. 2001. "While a Utility May Be Failing, Its Owner Is Not." *New York Times,* April 30: A1, A17.

Piller, Dan. 2002. "Confidence in Deregulation Declining as Problems Rise." *Dallas-Fort Worth Star Telegram,* June 9: 1.

Regens, James L. 1979. "State Responses to the Energy Issue: An Analysis of Innovation." *Social Science Quarterly* 61, no. 1: 44–57.

Rhode Island Public Utilities Commission. 2001. *Report of the Rhode Island Public Utilities Commission on Electric Restructuring,* February 28; available at: www.ripuc.org/energy/relegislature2001.pdf.

Saudi Arabian Information Resource. [n.d.] "Oil: Historical Background and Aramco;" available at: www.saudinf.com/main/d11.htm.

Savas, E.S. 1983. *Privatizing the Public Sector: How to Shrink Government.* Chatham, NJ: Chatham House.

Smeloff, Ed, and Peter Asmus. 1997. *Reinventing Electric Utilities: Competition, Citizen Action, and Clean Power.* Washington, DC: Island Press.

State of California. 2003. Energy Action Plan, May 8; available at: www.documents. dgs.ca.gov/cpa/joint/26305.pdf.

State of Wisconsin. 1986. *Governor's Energy Efficiency Plan.* Madison, WI: Department of Administration.

Timney, Mary M. 2002. "Short Circuit: Federal-State Relations in the California Energy Crisis." *Publius: The Journal of Federalism* 32: 109–22.

Tongren, Robert S. 2003. "Consumers' Counsel Calls for Regulatory Action to Spur Electric Competition and Protect Ohio Consumers." Ohio Consumers' Counsel. 2002 End-of-Year Update on Ohio's Electric Market; available at: www.pickocc. org/ news/182003.shtml (February 18, 2004).

U.S. Department of Energy. "The Budget for Fiscal Year 2003;" available at: www.energy.gov.

U.S. General Accounting Office. 2002. "Energy Markets: Concerted Actions Needed by FERC to Confront Challenges That Impede Effectiveness," GAO-02-656, June; available at: www.gao.gov.

Vietor, Richard H.K. 1984. *Energy Policy in America Since 1945: A Study of Business-Government Relations.* Cambridge: Cambridge University Press.

Viner, Jacob. 1927. "Adam Smith and Laissez Faire." *Journal of Political Economy* 35, no. 2: 198–232.

Weidenbaum, Murray L. 1981. *Business, Government, and the Public.* Englewood Cliffs, NJ: Prentice Hall.

Weingroff, Richard F. 2003. "Creating a Landmark: The Intermodal Surface Transportation Act of 1991." Federal Highway Administration, U.S. Department of Transportation, April 28; available at: www.fhwa.dot.gov/infrastructure/rw01.htm.

Witherspoon, Roger. 2003. "Report Says Public Can't Be Protected." *Journal News*, Westchester County, January 11: A1.

Further Reading

Bailey, Mary Timney. "An Innovative Management System for Improving Energy Conservation in Municipal Government Operations." Ph.D. dissertation. University of Pittsburgh, Graduate School of Public and International Affairs, 1984.

Baumol, William J., and J. Gregory Sidak. *Transmission Pricing and Stranded Costs in the Electric Power Industry.* Washington, DC: AEI Press, 1995.

Blair, Peter D. "U.S. Energy Policy Perspectives for the 1990s." In *Making National Energy Policy*, ed. Hans H. Landsberg, 7–40. Washington, DC: Resources for the Future, 1993.

Blumstein, Carl; Betsy Krieg; Lee Schipper; and Carl York. "Overcoming Social and Institutional Barriers to Energy Conservation." *Energy* 5 (1979): 355–71.

Cicchetti, Charles J., and John L. Jurewitz, eds. *Studies in Electric Utility Regulation.* Cambridge, MA: Ballinger, 1975.

Colle, Zachary. "$3.3 Billion Energy Overcharge FERC RULING: Federal Regulators Tally Short of Davis' Demands." *San Francisco Chronicle,* March 27, 2003. Available at www.sfgate.com.

Eisner, Marc Allen; Jeff Worsham; and Evan J. Ringquist. *Contemporary Regulatory Policy.* London: Lynne Rienner, 2000.

Heilbroner, Robert L. 1965. *The Worldly Philosophers: The Lives, Times, and Ideas of the Great Economic Thinkers.* New York: Simon and Schuster, 1965.

Jones, Bradford S. "State Responses to Global Climate Change." *Policy Studies Journal* 19, no. 2 (1991): 73–82.

King, Cheryl S., and Camilla Stivers, eds. *Government Is Us: Strategies for an Anti-Government Era.* Thousand Oaks, CA: Sage, 1998.

Landsberg, Hans H., ed. *Making National Energy Policy.* Washington, DC: Resources for the Future, 1993.

Maher, Ellen. "The Dynamics of Growth in the Electric Power Industry." In *Values in the Electric Power Industry*, ed. Kenneth Sayre, 149–216. Notre Dame, IN: University of Notre Dame Press, 1977.

Montgomery, W. David. "Interdependencies Between Energy and Environmental Policies." In *Making National Energy Policy*, ed. Hans H. Landsberg, 61–94. Washington, DC: Resources for the Future, 1993.

Portney, Paul R., ed. *Natural Resources and the Environment: The Reagan Approach.* Washington, DC: Urban Institute Press, 1984.

Sawhill, John C., ed. *Energy Conservation and Public Policy.* Englewood Cliffs, NJ: Prentice-Hall, 1979.

Sayre, Kenneth, ed. *Values in the Electric Power Industry.* Notre Dame, IN: University of Notre Dame Press, 1977.

Sclove, Richard E. "Energy Policy and Democratic Theory." In *Uncertain Power: The Struggle for a National Energy Policy,* ed. Dorothy S. Zinberg, 37–65. Elmsford, NY: Pergamon Press, 1983.

Smith, Vernon L. "Can Electric Power—A 'Natural Monopoly'—Be Deregulated?" In *Making National Energy Policy,* ed. Hans H. Landsberg, 131–51. Washington, DC: Resources for the Future, 1993.

Sunstein, Cass R. *After the Rights Revolution: Reconceiving the Regulatory State.* Cambridge, MA: Harvard University Press, 1990.

Thayer, Frederick C. *An End to Hierarchy and Competition.* 2d ed. New York: Franklin Watts, 1981.

Timney, Mary M. "Eco-Nomics: Toward a Theory of Value for Public Administration." *Administrative Theory & Praxis* 23 (2001): 25–28.

Vietor, Richard H.K. *Contrived Competition: Regulation and Deregulation in America.* Cambridge, MA: Belknap Press of Harvard University Press, 1994.

Waring, Marilyn. *If Women Counted.* San Francisco: Harper and Row, 1988.

Zinberg, Dorothy S., ed. *Uncertain Power: The Struggle for a National Energy Policy.* Elmsford, NY: Pergamon Press, 1983.

Index

About the Author

Mary M. Timney is chair of the Department of Political Science at Pace University. For five years, she was professor of Public Administration at California State University, Hayward, where she experienced the California electricity crisis firsthand. She has also been on the faculties of the University of Cincinnati and the University of Wisconsin-Green Bay. She holds an AB in chemistry from Bryn Mawr College and Master of Public Administration and Ph.D. in Public and International Affairs from the University of Pittsburgh.

An activist in the environmental movement of the 1970s in Pittsburgh, she was environmental research associate for the Western Pennsylvania Conservancy. Later, as executive director of the Allegheny County Environmental Coalition, she implemented two grants from the U.S. Environmental Protection Agency and developed public education programs on transportation control strategies. While completing her Ph.D. in the early 1980s, she worked as energy project director in the city of Pittsburgh mayor's office and designed an energy program budgeting system. In 1985, the governor of Wisconsin appointed her to a special task force to develop an energy policy plan. This work served as the base for a funded research project to investigate the development of state energy policies during the 1980s in the absence of federal energy policy leadership.

Timney's research and teaching interests are environmental policy, including environmental justice and sustainable development; public budgeting, public administration theory, and ethics; and public participation.